Ideas and Action Series, No. 1

W.W. Rostow
Pre-Invasion Bombing Strategy

General Eisenhower's Decision of March 25, 1944

 University of Texas Press, Austin

Copyright © 1981 by the University of Texas Press
All rights reserved
Printed in the United States of America

First Edition, 1981

Requests for permission to reproduce material from this work
should be sent to
Permissions, University of Texas Press
Box 7819
Austin, Texas 78712

Library of Congress Cataloging in Publication Data
Rostow, Walt Whitman, 1916–
  Pre-invasion bombing strategy.
  (Ideas and action series; no. 1)
  Includes bibliographical references.
  1. Operation Overlord. 2. World War, 1939–1945—Destruction and
pillage—Germany. 3. World War, 1939–1945—Aerial operations.
4. World War, 1939–1945—Economic aspects—Germany.
5. Deployment strategy. 6. Eisenhower, Dwight David, Pres. U.S.,
1890–1969. I. Title. II. Series.
D756.5.N6R64   940.54′42   80-28002
ISBN 0-292-76470-7
ISBN 0-292-76471-5 (pbk.)

In memory of
Richard D'Oyly Hughes

Contents

Preface ix

1. The Apparent Choices and the Decision   3
2. Zuckerman's Theory: The Strategic Attack on Transport for Tactical Purposes   7
3. EOU and Its Doctrine   15
4. The Winning of Daylight Air Supremacy over Germany   24
5. The Choice of Oil and Its Initial Defeat   31
6. EOU Goes Tactical   36
7. The Arena of Decision: Power, Vested Interest, and Personality   44
8. How Oil and Bridges Got In   52
9. The Neoclassical Period: September 1944–May 1945   66
10. A Few Conclusions   72

Appendixes

A. Final Minutes of the March 25 Meeting   88
B. The EOU Doctrine: Four Memoranda   99
C. Spaatz-Eisenhower Memorandum of March 31, 1944   113
D. Report on the May 7, 1944, Destruction of the Bridge at Vernon   116
E. Bombing Policy on the Eve of the Battle of the Bulge: Memorandum of W. W. Rostow, December 6, 1944   119
F. German Rail Movement in France in the First Ten Days after D-Day: An Interim Report by Charles P. Kindleberger, June 16–19, 1944   122

Notes   139   Index   159

Tables

1. German Single-Engine Fighter Aircraft Acceptances, 1943 27
2. Monthly German Production and Imports of Total Finished Oil Products and Aircraft Fuel, January 1944–March 1945 68

Preface

In counterpoint to my work as an economist and economic historian, I am launched into a leisurely effort to explore the relationship between ideas and action. By ideas I mean the abstract concepts that public officials and their advisers bring to bear in making decisions. My experiences as both an academic and a public servant have equally driven home over the years this piece of wisdom in George Santayana's *Character and Opinion in the United States*: ". . . human discourse is intrinsically addressed not to natural existing things but to ideal essences, poetic or logical terms which thought may define and play with. When fortune or necessity diverts our attention from this congenial ideal sport to crude facts and pressing issues, we turn our frail poetic ideas into symbols for those terrible irruptive things. In that paper money of our own stamping, the legal tender of the mind, we are obliged to reckon all the movements and values of the world."

But there is, of course, a good deal more to decisions in public policy than clash and choice among the "frail poetic ideas" we create to make simplified sense of an inordinately complex and usually disheveled field of action. A decision is, after all, a choice among perceived alternatives. Ideas play a large role in defining those alternatives; but the choice among them involves other factors. The precise setting and timing of the decision evidently matter. So do questions of power, that is, politics and bureaucratic vested interests. So do personalities—unique human beings, controlled by memories and experiences, dreams and hopes, which James Gould Cozzens evoked, in *By Love Possessed*, in a definition of temperament: "A man's temperament might, perhaps, be defined as the mode or modes of a man's feeling, the struck balance of his ruling desires, the worked-out sum of his habitual predispositions. In themselves, these elements were inscrutable. There were usually too many of them; they were often of irreducible complexity; you could observe only results. . . . The to-be-observed result was a total way of life."

In this effort to illuminate the relationship between ideas and action, I decided to proceed as follows. First, to examine a series of eight or nine specific decisions taken by particular high public officials at particular times. In each case, the decision would be briefly described, including the options which the executive perceived as available; the conceptual debate involved in the decision—the more or less pure intellectual content of the process—would be delineated; the larger background of events would be evoked; the interplay of the conceptual debate and the other, more mundane forces in play would be examined; the follow-on events and consequences of the decision would be weighed. Along the way an effort would be made to capture the odd, often adventitious circumstances which entered into the decision and into the way things actually turned out. There are strands of accident and even humor—high, low, or wry—running through a good many of these case studies as well as pratfalls from which even the highest officials are not exempt. Indeed, this is a built-in hazard of the human condition because decisions are almost always made with imperfect information and foresight, involving a step into the dark. In this essay we are literally dealing with men groping through "the fog of war"; but the image is equally apt for decisions in diplomacy or domestic policy.

I have chosen to examine decisions in which I played some

role or which I had an opportunity to observe closely at the time. But, as the reader will perceive, this and the other essays are not exercises in autobiography. It is simply the case that one has a better chance of capturing something of the relationship between ideas and the other elements determining action if one was reasonably close to events than if the whole complex setting has to be reconstructed from the beginning.

On the other hand, my memory of the circumstances, the material in my files, and my knowledge of some of the actors were patently inadequate. In this and the other case studies, my purpose is to bring to bear what public records, communication with participants, and the literature of published memoirs and works of scholarship can now provide. As in the present essay, there is usually a formidable body of relevant material available.

My first notion was to include these case studies within a single volume. Although I tried to keep them relatively brief, it soon became apparent that it would be impossible to render a reasonably coherent account of each decision within the compass of a chapter of conventional length. I accepted, therefore, the suggestion of the University of Texas Press that the case studies be published as a series of short books. This method has the advantage of permitting the presentation, in appendixes, of selected source or other basic materials hitherto unpublished or not easily accessible which illuminate facets of the decision or capture something of the moods and temper of the time.

As we put this first essay in the series to press, several further case studies are nearing completion or are firmly planned:

— *An All European Settlement?* Secretary Byrnes' Decision of April 20, 1946.
— *Should the U.S. Initiate Negotiations in the Wake of Stalin's Death?* President Eisenhower's Decision of March 11, 1953.

— *Open Skies*: President Eisenhower's Decision of July 21, 1955.
— *Aid to India and Pakistan*: The Launching of the Kennedy-Cooper Resolution on March 25, 1958.
— *Asian Regionalism*: President Johnson's Decisions of 1965–1966.

In addition, I plan to select a major U.S. decision on energy policy in the period 1977–1980 and one on the emergence of supply-side economics in 1979–1980. I have not yet decided among a number of other possible decisions of the 1960's. The problem I confront with this period is that I have already written in some detail about the major decisions of the presidents in *The Diffusion of Power*.

I plan to conclude the series with an extended general essay on the theme of ideas and action, reflecting on the cases examined but drawing also on a much wider historical and analytic literature.

In writing this essay, on one of the most intensely debated issues of the Second World War, I consulted a good many participants in the events described, scholars of World War II, and others whose knowledge or insight might be helpful. They, as well as archivists, were uniformly helpful; and I wish to acknowledge their generous assistance: Bernard Babington Smith; Constance Babington Smith; Harold J. Barnett; Martin Blumenson; Ted Carpenter; Lloyd Cornett; Ira C. Eaker; James N. Eastman, Jr.; John S. D. Eisenhower; Derek Ezra; Stanley Falk; Noble Frankland; Alfred Goldberg; Andrew J. Goodpaster; Haywood S. Hansell; Mrs. W. Averell Harriman; Mrs. Richard D'Oyly Hughes; Ira Iscoe; R. V. Jones; Carl Kaysen; Charles P. Kindleberger; F. F. Lambert; Clarence Lasby; Henry D. Lytton; Edward S. Mason; Harry Middleton; Robert V. Roosa; Eugene V. Rostow; F. M. Sallagar; the late Frederic H. Smith, Jr.; John E. Taylor; E. H. Turner; Henry H. Villard; William F. Whitmore; Solly Zuckerman.

As on many other occasions, I was aided in multiple ways

by Lois Nivens. Frances Knape was most helpful in typing the various drafts.

I should add that this enterprise would not have been undertaken without the strong encouragement of my wife, Elspeth Davies Rostow, who believed I might usefully reflect on the large central question embedded in those periods in my professional life when I was diverted from strictly academic pursuits.

W. W. Rostow

November 1980
Austin, Texas

Pre-Invasion Bombing Strategy
General Eisenhower's Decision of March 25, 1944

1. The Apparent Choices and the Decision

On Saturday afternoon, March 25, 1944, General Dwight D. Eisenhower met at the Air Ministry in London with all the major military figures in Britain directly concerned with the application of air power against Germany.[1] Charles Portal, chief of the British Air Staff (CAS) and a member of the Combined Chiefs of Staff, chaired the session; but, implicitly at least, Dwight Eisenhower's was the deciding voice. Also present were Arthur Tedder, Eisenhower's deputy in command of OVERLORD in the Supreme Headquarters Allied Expeditionary Force (SHAEF); Carl Spaatz, commander of the U.S. Strategic Air Forces in Europe (USSTAF), and his influential deputy, Frederick Anderson; Arthur Harris, chief of RAF Bomber Command; Trafford Leigh-Mallory, commander of the Allied Expeditionary Air Force (AEAF), made up of tactical aircraft grouped in support of the forthcoming invasion. Representatives of the War Office, the Joint Intelligence Staff (JIS), and the Ministry of Economic Warfare (MEW) were also present. The text of the official minutes of the meeting is given in Appendix A.

The issue was: How should the massive British and American bombing forces be employed in the two months before D-Day and in the period immediately thereafter to maximize the chance that a bridgehead would be successfully established and the allied forces built up for a successful break-out? On the face of it, the choice, as it was laid before

Eisenhower, was simple: a systematic assault on the railway centers (marshalling yards and rail repair facilities) of northwestern Europe or a systematic attack on German oil production. The major protagonists were Tedder and Spaatz, although Harris also took a distinctive position. Tedder argued that the systematic devastation of the rail facilities of northwestern Europe would delay and hinder the movement of German reinforcements and supplies and was, therefore, the optimum method for assuring the success of the invasion. Spaatz argued that attacks on German oil production represented the optimum use of strategic air power, including the attrition that could be imposed on the Luftwaffe, the German air force. He judged that the Luftwaffe would rise to defend the oil plants but would not expend its scarce single-engine fighter force to defend what he regarded as the second-order targets represented by Tedder's plan for attacking railway centers. Harris argued for the primacy of the continued area assault on German cities, in which the RAF Bomber Command had long been engaged, doubted that his command could operate against the transport targets with sufficient precision to be effective, and cited the high level of civilian casualties that Tedder's transport plan was likely to impose on friends in occupied territories.

British War Office, intelligence, and economic warfare experts expressed grave doubts that the Tedder plan would produce major direct military effects, in part on the basis of experience in Italy with marshalling-yard attacks. But Eisenhower decided, with Portal's support, to adopt the transport plan on the grounds that "it was only necessary to show that there would be *some* reduction, however small, to justify adopting the plan, provided that there was no alternative available." The alternative presented was Spaatz' oil plan; but the oil experts appeared to agree that German stocks of oil were such that the effects of an attack on oil production on German military capabilities would be delayed up to four or five months, whereas Eisenhower was focused on the period from D-Day to D plus 30. On the other hand, Eisenhower judged that the overriding task for allied strategic air power was to assure air supremacy over the continental battlefield—a caveat that was to assume significance in subsequent weeks. The decision in favor of the transport plan was formally made on March 26.

With Portal's backing, Eisenhower appeared to have settled a critical issue which had been argued at length and with some passion since the arrival in England of Eisenhower and Tedder in January. In fact, the positions brought to the March 25 meeting and Eisenhower's decision were more complex than this brisk preliminary summary would suggest; it was not until April 17 that Eisenhower's decision at the military level was rendered definitive; and it took a further three weeks before Prime Minister Winston Churchill's grave doubts were overruled, in effect, by Eisenhower, backed, in turn, by General George Marshall and President Franklin Roosevelt. As we shall see, the attack on oil had been slipped in through the back door as early as April 5. And a month before D-Day the initial concept that lay behind the transport plan was significantly modified to include a systematic attack on the Seine and other bridges, a potential alternative to the marshalling-yard attacks which, for reasons which will emerge, was not laid before Eisenhower at the March 25 meeting.

By and large, however, the formal directive issued by Eisenhower to Spaatz and Harris on April 17, 1944, appeared to confirm the priorities he had established at the meeting of March 25:

> OVERALL MISSION
> 1. . . . Our re-entry on the Continent constitutes the supreme operation for 1944; all possible support must, therefore, be afforded to the Allied Armies by our Air Forces to assist them in establishing themselves in the lodgment area.

PARTICULAR MISSION

2. The first pre-requisite of success in the maintenance of the combined bomber offensive and of our re-entry on the Continent is an overall reduction of the enemy's air combat strength and particularly his air fighter strength. The primary role of our Air Forces in the European and Mediterranean theaters is, therefore, to secure and maintain air superiority.

3. Our armies will also require the maximum possible assistance on the ground preparatory to the actual assault. This can best be given by interfering with rail communications in the "OVERLORD" area. . . .

4. The particular mission of the strategical air forces prior to the "OVERLORD" assault is:
    (a) To deplete the German air force and particularly the German fighter forces, and to destroy and disorganize the facilities supporting them.
    (b) To destroy and disrupt the enemy's rail communications, particularly those affecting the enemy's movement towards the "OVERLORD" lodgment area.[2]

The primacy accorded the maintenance of air supremacy provided some flexibility to Spaatz, but he appeared to be flatly denied the right to attack oil targets. Harris, in this directive, was also given some flexibility to continue to bomb German cities on the incorrect grounds that RAF Bomber Command's capacity to strike precise targets was more limited than that of the American bombers; but he was also instructed to coordinate, "where tactical conditions allow," on German air force and rail communication targets.

2. Zuckerman's Theory: The Strategic Attack on Transport for Tactical Purposes

To sort out these matters, it may be well to begin with the intellectual content of the debate. As always, there was a great deal more to a controversy of this kind and its interim resolution than intellectual argument. But, as always, competing concepts were also embedded in the debate. In terms of concept, the debate on March 25 brought to a head two strikingly different notions of the principles on which strategic and tactical bombing should be based—with Harris' theory of area bombing present, but not at this time on center stage.

First, there were the concepts developed by the apparent intellectual victor of March 25, Solly Zuckerman, strongly backed by Tedder and Leigh-Mallory. In his *From Apes to Warlords,* Zuckerman provides a detailed account of his career, the evolution of his ideas, and the bureaucratic battle of 1944 as he perceived it at the time and in retrospect. His intellectual progression in matters relating to bombing and bombing policy is interwoven with a narrative of personal events and personalities, but it can be set out as follows.

Shortly after the outbreak of war in 1939, Zuckerman was recruited to work at the Research and Experiments Department of the Ministry of Home Security, located at Princes Risborough. His task was to establish whether there was any risk that people in underground home shelters might suffer from concussion as the result of shock waves which passed through the earth when a bomb exploded nearby. Trained as a doctor, he had, in fact, not practiced medicine but studied the sexual and social life of apes and monkeys, publishing two books on this theme. In 1934 he became a research fellow and university lecturer in the Anatomy Department at Oxford. Against this background, it was natural for Zuckerman to use monkeys—and, later, other laboratory animals—to establish, in controlled experiments, the physical effects of blast and high-velocity fragments.

This experimental work widened, in 1940–1942, into broader analyses of German raids on Britain, including, especially, an analysis of the physical and morale effects of the German attacks on Birmingham and Hull. These studies involved analyses of the effects of bombs of different sizes and fusing and the relative efficacy of high explosives versus incendiaries in attacks on housing and factories. The findings were drawn into the debate on the potentialities of area bombing of cities in Germany and the 1942 decision to pursue this strategy—a decision from which Zuckerman takes his distance.

A brief tour in Louis Mountbatten's Combined Operations brought Zuckerman still closer to Allied operations as opposed to the results of German operations. First, he was drawn into the design of an operation to assault the island of Alderney, in the Channel some ten miles west of the tip of the Cherbourg peninsula. His task was to organize a plan for the silencing of the German artillery batteries. Given normal aiming errors, guns were hard to hit directly even with attacks of great density. In calculating required bomb density, Zuckerman came up with an "arbitrary criterion" that collateral damage would take out two guns for every one directly hit, and he sought to estimate the morale effects on the German forces of attacks of the proposed density. The assault was abandoned; but the two concepts evolved in this exercise—the effects on enemy capabilities, beyond direct destruction, of collateral damage and of reduced morale—directly affected Zuckerman's planning of the attack on Pantelleria and suffused also his later assessment of the potentialities of attacks on rail facilities in Italy and Western Europe. Second, it was from Combined Operations that Zuckerman was sent out to Cairo in January 1943 to investigate how, despite British air supremacy over the battlefield, Field Marshal Erwin Rommel had managed to retreat with some success from his defeat at El Alamein. On the spot, Zuckerman's mission was transformed into an assessment of Allied bombing operations against Tripoli. He recommended altered fusing of bombs, improvements in the destructive power of British bombs, and greater use of smaller rather than larger bombs. But most important of all, Zuckerman met Tedder and evidently impressed him favorably. After a brief return to London, Zuckerman was ordered back to North Africa where he joined Tedder's staff as scientific adviser, a status in which he remained, with some additional responsibilities, for the duration of the war.

Zuckerman soon found himself in Algiers where he was designated a planner for the assault on the island of Pantelleria. Although a landing by Allied forces was envisaged, if necessary, the hope was to induce the surrender of the Italian garrison by the concentrated application of air power, supplemented by naval bombardment. Zuckerman's plan drew on each of the strands in his prior experience and the lessons he drew from them. It derived, quite particularly, from the design for the aborted operation on Alderney; but his prior conclusions about appropriate bomb size and fusing were also reflected. He urged concentration on the guns at the north end of the island where landings were envisaged and recommended a density of attack sufficient to destroy about one-third of the batteries, counting on secondary effects to render the rest nonoperational. He noted the likelihood of significant morale effects.

The Italian commander did, indeed, surrender just before the planned assault from landing craft.

Pantelleria is an island about nine miles long, six miles wide. Its air power was eliminated at an early stage. Its garrison of twelve thousand was, in effect, isolated and virtually defenseless against massive bombardment, including some five hundred U.S. B-17 bombers. Most of the six hundred Germans on the island were withdrawn at the beginning of the air offensive. It is not surprising that, under these unique circumstances, the Italian commander felt he could honorably surrender after three weeks of bombardment, the latter twelve days of which were extremely heavy.

Zuckerman's calculations of the probable damage to the batteries proved reasonably accurate, and the success of the operation as a whole elevated his prestige in target planning. Tedder feared and Zuckerman acknowledged that excessively broad lessons might be drawn from the special advantageous circumstances of the Pantelleria exercise.

It was logical, however, that Zuckerman should be asked to contribute his advice on air operations in support of the forthcoming assault on Sicily. Here is how he describes his position, introducing the anti-interdiction theme which runs through his position for the rest of the war in Europe, postwar evaluations of bombing policy, down to his autobiography and beyond.

> When Tedder had first asked me to give him my ideas about what bombing operations should precede the invasion of Sicily, I had suggested a plan to destroy the rail and road communications on which the enemy depended. It departed from an earlier and official appreciation that had been put forward on 4 June by the Intelligence Staff of the Northwest African Tactical Air Force, and which proposed as "targets of choice" the bombing of railway lines at points where they could not easily be repaired. This plan also advocated the creation of road blocks by the bombing of small towns through which "strategic" roads ran. The plan that I suggested focused on the destruction of the nodal points which controlled the railway system of Sicily and Southern Italy.[5]

Zuckerman does not explain when and how he came to focus on the bombing of transport centers in support of ground operations and how he came to the judgment that generalized destruction of such facilities would yield tactical results superior to interdiction; but, on his own account, he held before the event the view he was to elaborate in the evaluation of the results of the 1943 bombing in Sicily and the Italian mainland, with which Tedder entrusted him.

It is perhaps permissible to deduce, from Zuckerman's experience, that his attraction to marshalling yards related to his work on the physical effects of bombing. Here were large targets, often large enough to contain the whole bombing pattern of an attacking force. The target was filled with tracks and contained often a good many cars and engines as well as repair facilities. From a physical point of view, fewer bombs were wasted than on smaller targets where direct hits at key physical points were necessary for a useful result. As late as June 1979 Zuckerman states what may have been, for him, the controlling insight: "Only a direct hit counted on a bridge, whereas any bomb on a railway centre caused damage."[4] It was not difficult to believe that the protracted attack on such targets would have significant and cumulative, if diffuse, effects on the enemy's capacity to conduct military operations, even if military traffic was a small percentage of total traffic. And from the earliest British and American planning, such transport targets had been seriously considered among the options examined. Indeed, as a strategic system, German transport was included in both the first of the American strategic bombing plans (AWPD-1) and the Casablanca directive of January 1943. But long before the issue became inflamed, some, on balance, came to the conclusion that, despite their evident attractions, marshalling yards were not an optimum target system either to prevent enemy forces and supplies from moving to the front or for reducing overall German military capabilities.

The evaluation of transport bombing in the Sicily campaign

was dated December 28, 1943, that is, the eve of the shift of the Mediterranean team to Britain. The Sicily Report, in subsequent months and in Zuckerman's autobiography, is cited as the primary empirical basis for the proposition he subsequently applied to northwestern Europe. Its general conclusions include these passages:

> The strategical effect of destroying the enemy's means of rail communication is best achieved by attacks on large railway centres which contain important repair facilities and large concentrations of locomotives and rolling-stock. The sub-targets (e.g. tracks, rolling-stock, warehouses, repair sheds, etc.) in a large railway area are very concentrated. As a result, the general risk of damage from bombing, if the attacks are carried out in adequate strength, is very high.
> The efficiency of a railway system appears to fall very rapidly when bombing simultaneously leads to an increase in the calls upon, and a decrease in the capacity of the repair facilities. . . .
> A far more costly air effort would be needed to achieve a tactical success, in the sense of a sudden blocking of communications at any given series of points, than has proved necessary to produce the strategical effect of reducing traffic potential by the destruction of rolling-stock and repair facilities.[5]

The special conclusions of the Sicily Report included this terse sentence which, like a theme in a symphony, was to be greatly elaborated: "Railway and road bridges are uneconomical and difficult targets, and in general do not appear to be worth attacking except where special considerations demand it in the tactical area."

Zuckerman's evaluation of evidence bearing on the Sicilian campaign and the transport bombing of the Italian mainland was to be seriously challenged both in the Mediterranean and in London (see below, pp. 38–41 and 56–60), although his autobiography states that he had never "heard anyone criticizing the factual analysis which I had made of the breakdown of railway communications in Southern Italy and Sicily."[6]

On arrival in England at the turn of the year, Zuckerman was assigned formally to assist Leigh-Mallory, who had been appointed commander of the AEAF. For reasons not relevant here, Leigh-Mallory never acquired the authority his post appeared to grant. Tedder, as Eisenhower's deputy, carried the brunt of the battle for the transportation plan, and Zuckerman continued to work closely with him, as scientific adviser to both commanders.

Zuckerman found that a tactical air support plan had been drawn up in 1943 by those engaged in preliminary planning for OVERLORD. In concept it was similar to the initial plan drawn up for the invasion of Sicily which Zuckerman had opposed. It called for sustained attacks before D-Day, designed to isolate the battlefield in the limited sense of forcing German support forces to detrain a considerable distance from the coast. Zuckerman reports his reaction in terms which are almost identical to his reaction to the preliminary plan for the support of the invasion of Sicily:

> Kingston [author of the preliminary plan for OVERLORD] accepted my immediate comment that it would be hazardous in the extreme to rely on good flying weather in the two to three weeks before the proposed date of the assault, and on the very precise bombing operations which the plan demanded. I also expressed doubts about the ability of our fighter-bombers to cut railway lines and destroy tunnels and bridges in order to force the enemy to detrain some hundred miles from the assault area. Kingston was also ready to believe, what Italian experience had revealed, that the desired disruption of communications could be more securely achieved by a "strategic" attack on the railway network than by any attempt to cut it at specific points. We therefore agreed that the moment I got back to London I would prepare an alternative plan which he would then submit to Leigh-Mallory.[7]

This doctrine of strategic, attritional attack on rail facilities for tactical purposes was incorporated in an AEAF planning paper of January 22, 1944, "Delay and Disorganization of Enemy Movement by Rail."[8] Zuckerman was the principal author. The paper called for attack on the seventy-six most important servicing and repair facilities in northwestern Europe; promised to "paralyze movement in the whole region they serve and render almost impossible the subsequent movement by rail of major reserves into France"; and foreshadowed Zuckerman's post–D-Day advocacy of the assault on German railroads as a strategic target system, successful attack on which would reduce German war production.

The paper estimated that the pre–D-Day bombing of rail centers would require less than half the capabilities of RAF Bomber Command and well over half of the U.S. strategic bombing force.

The backing of this plan by Leigh-Mallory and Tedder detonated more than eleven weeks of intense controversy, reaching the highest levels of the British and American governments, settled ad interim by Eisenhower on March 25, formally on April 17, politically as late as May 11 when, in fact, the attack on the French railway centers was well advanced.

3. EOU and Its Doctrine

In describing now the intellectual basis for the views which constituted the main opposition to Zuckerman's propositions, I shall focus primarily on the Enemy Objectives Unit (EOU) of the Economic Warfare Division of the U.S. Embassy in London. But several elements of asymmetry should be noted. First, Zuckerman operated as an individual, although he was provided with and supported by a considerable staff. But neither at the time nor from Zuckerman's autobiography does one get the feeling that the staff engaged in much internal debate or self-criticism. Zuckerman clearly dominated his staff—an observation which in no way prejudges the quality of the advice ultimately rendered.

Zuckerman had come into the target-selection business in a tactical theater; and in dealing with Tedder and Leigh-Mallory, he was engaged with men, like himself, whose careers had never required them to formulate criteria for target selection in a strategic context and to apply them systematically by comparison of alternative target systems. Leigh-Mallory had risen as a commander of fighter units. Tedder's background was more complex: pilot training, a Singapore air command, aircraft and air armaments research and development, and three years in the Middle East starting in November 1940.[9] There his task was air support of the ground campaigns that began on the approaches to Cairo and ended at the close of 1943 with the Allied ground forces in southern Italy as he and Eisenhower were transferred to London.

The position of EOU differed from Zuckerman's in three distinct respects: EOU was a team of equals whose like-mindedness evolved from a continuing process of internal debate from September 1942 onward; it was also part of the larger Anglo-American intelligence and planning community centered in London; and it developed close ties to the leaders of the U.S. Army Air Forces and the Air Ministry planners who had lived intimately with the problems of target planning in the painful passage from a desperately defensive posture in the Battle of Britain to the achievement of air dominance over Germany in February 1944.

In the first instance, EOU was linked closely to and, de facto, became a target planning staff for the American bomber forces in Europe. The Army Air Forces had made an early commitment to daylight precision bombing. Therefore, criteria had to be developed for the selection of one target system versus another, one target within a system versus another, and, if the target was large enough and bombing precise enough, one aiming point versus another. The intellectual level of development of these criteria was quite primitive when EOU was set up in London in September 1942. But the Air Force officers with whom EOU worked were deeply indoctrinated in the relevance of this array of questions. The scale and composition of the Army Air Forces, as well as U.S. aircraft production targets, were determined, in a rather remarkable tour de force, on the basis of AWPD-1 (Air War Plans Division—Plan 1). That plan was hastily, but not thoughtlessly, devised in 1941, substantially shaped by a specification of the target systems whose destruction was required to assure German defeat.[10] Colonel Richard D'Oyly Hughes, one of the participants in the construction of AWPD-1, became the senior target planning officer for the U.S. Air Forces in Europe, the principal link between EOU and U.S. bombing forces in Europe over the critical period from September 1942 to the full establishment of Allied forces on the Continent in 1944.

Hughes, somewhere, deserves a chapter of his own. A British army officer who had become an American citizen in the early 1930's, he was one of those selfless men, of high intelligence, integrity, and dedication, who play major roles in great enterprises but, operating at a middle level of authority, leave little trace in the formal records of history.[11]

Hughes was, in fact, the father of EOU. In 1942 he found himself in London, wholly dependent on British sources of intelligence, without an independent staff capable of evaluating the flow of material on which planning had to be based. He induced Ambassador John G. Winant to request that appropriately trained staff be sent to London to work, in fact, for Hughes, but formally within the embassy.[12] After some bureaucratic infighting, the Office of Strategic Services (OSS) and the Board of Economic Warfare (BEW) combined to supply the staff that was needed. The first contingent, consisting of Chandler Morse, the unit's chief, Roselene Honerkamp, its secretary, and me, arrived in London on September 13, 1942. At peak strength in London before D-Day, the professional staff of EOU consisted of ten men, of whom two were assigned to the Air Ministry, plus one assigned to the Mediterranean.

The previous experience of those who served EOU and its outposts over the subsequent thirty-two months converged in a quite particular way with Hughes' intellectual biases. As a professional soldier he had long been trained in the principles of concentration of effort at the enemy's most vulnerable point and of maximum follow-through when a breakthrough was achieved. And, for a curious reason, he had thought, long before the rest of us, about the appropriate principles that should govern bombing policy. He had carried with him, as a British army officer, and kept under his pillow at night a book by Ernest Swinton, *The Green Curve*. Swinton, a British staff officer, is remembered in history as the inventor of the tank in the First World War, whose creative zeal was initially frustrated by the War Office, to be salvaged, after a tragic delay, by Winston Churchill at the Admiralty—a fact for which the War Office never forgave Swinton. *The Green Curve* consists of a series of vividly evoked abstract military situations, each illustrating a basic principle. One chapter, "The Joint in the Harness," was initially published in January 1907, three years after the Wright brothers' first successful flight. It envisaged bombing aircraft and a situation in which, after alternatives are canvassed, a pile driver is chosen as the appropriate aiming point to delay the building of a bridge on which the flow of supplies to an army depends. At the head of the story is this evocation of the pure theory of interdiction: "Railways are the arteries of modern armies. Vitality decreases when they are blocked, and terminates when they are permanently severed" (*Imperial Strategy*, 1906).

In any case, Hughes fathered EOU, guided it, used it, and formed a critical link to Fred Anderson and, later, Carl Spaatz, both of whom some EOU members came to know well.

But with Hughes' encouragement, the ties of EOU members and their channels of communication reached out all over London and, before the war was over, beyond.[13] The ties built up, for example, between EOU and Sidney Bufton and Arthur Morley of the British Air Staff (Bomber Operations) in Whitehall and with Oliver Lawrence at MEW were as close in many ways as those to the American planners. And, when some members dispersed, as indicated in note 13, we developed collegial ties with our British and American colleagues, as well as independent channels of communication. The dispersal, which implanted our common doctrine into a number of different Allied staffs, we called Operation Octopus. We maintained close communications with one another throughout this faintly conspiratorial effort.

The British Air Staff and MEW had built their original bombing concepts around the notion of systematic attack on particular industries of the highest relevance to German military potential in the field. The capacity of the RAF, however, proved insufficient to conduct such attacks with the requisite weight, accuracy, and continuity of effort. Of necessity, RAF Bomber Command fell back to area bombing at night, that is, attacks on large urban areas. And, as British industry began to supply an enlarged flow of bombers built for this purpose, its capabilities increased. By early March 1943, a formidable array of technical problems had been overcome, permitting both improved accuracy and improved defense against German night fighters; and the systematic attack on the cities of the Ruhr began. At the end of July came the intense raids on Hamburg, marking, in a sense, the high point of RAF Bomber Command's attack on German cities. The British intelligence and planning staffs, outside RAF Bomber Command, while respecting the great courage and resourcefulness of the area bombing effort, regarded it as diffuse and indecisive in its effects on German war production, military strength in the field, and morale. They looked to the day when more precise and systematic attacks could be mounted, by British as well as American forces, on target systems of the highest priority. There was, then, an intellectual and conceptual convergence of American and British thought despite the understandable dissidence of Harris, who redoubtedly held to the view that Bomber Command's attacks on cities were the most profitable use of air power for the time.

EOU came at this set of problems from a somewhat different background and perspective than did the U.S. Army Air Forces planners, the RAF staff in Whitehall, or MEW. We were, by and large, trained as economists. We had joined OSS or BEW in 1941 or 1942. The OSS contingent came from the economic section of the Research and Analysis branch, headed by Edward S. Mason, a professor at Harvard. Although Mason had written relatively little, I believe it is fair to say that his qualities of judgment and character, combined with thoroughly professional skills, made him the most respected single figure among American economists—certainly among those who bridged the worlds of academic and public affairs.

He worked us hard, held us to high standards, and occasionally let his pleasure shine through at our ability to cope with rather odd tasks.

The earliest work done by the OSS economists was not on bombing policy, but it included three exercises which proved a useful background for EOU's later target work in London. They were studies of the logistical problems involved in a possible German invasion of French territory in northwestern Africa, an analysis which formed part of the foundations for planning the 1942 Allied landings in that region; the anticipated German thrust in the spring of 1942 through southern Russia to Stalingrad, a study in which the OSS analysts concluded correctly that the German situation would become progressively more precarious unless Voronezh and the double-track line to Stalingrad were captured; the supply possibilities and limitations of the Japanese offensive in the southwestern Pacific, with special attention to the Japanese capacity to secure a landing in Australia. All three of these studies required detailed analysis of the scale and character of supply requirements, under combat conditions of varying intensity, as well as close attention to the carrying capacity of roads, railway lines, and ships.

As note 13 indicates, EOU was initially put to work by Hughes not on high-flown theories of target selection but on a task as narrowly focused and painstaking as the logistical studies done in Washington: aiming-point reports. These were analyses of particular German industrial plants or installations designed to establish the most vulnerable point of attack. The reports were to be accompanied by a text which would state:

> a. The effect on the plant if the vulnerable point is destroyed;
>
> b. How long it is likely to take to effect repairs;
>
> c. The effect on the German war potential if the plant is out of action to the extent given in (a) for the period given in (b).[14]

The aiming-point reports were an invaluable education, requiring, among other things, visits to the nearest equivalent plants in Britain, as well as detailed exploitation of virtually all the intelligence London could provide. (The qualifier is necessary because EOU as an institution never had access to ULTRA, although I at the Air Ministry, Charles P. Kindleberger at Twenty-first [and then Twelfth] Army Group, and perhaps others who dispersed from 40 Berkeley Square, may have been introduced to its erratic but remarkable mysteries.)

Some 285 aiming-point reports were produced by EOU. They were useful intelligence summaries and were exploited as such by the Eighth and Fifteenth Air Force Bomber Commands (and occasionally by the RAF) both for general purposes and in setting operational aiming points for attack. They supplied, as well, a necessary foundation for damage assessment, since they indicated, within the limits of intelligence, which installations could be regarded as vital. They served, finally, as a guide to prisoner of war interrogators in the collection of further intelligence. More broadly, they established a concrete form for organizing intelligence for precision bombing purposes and a mode of thinking systematically and comparatively about precise targets. At the time they were introduced, no such detailed analyses were being done. British intelligence regarded the EOU interest in particular buildings as an evidence of undue optimism and even of faint morbidity. In a sense, that scepticism was justified, for precision bombing as carried out by the American heavy bombers was, in fact, pattern bombing. Only in the case of a few targets (e.g., synthetic oil plants) was the plant area larger than the minimum bomb pattern, so that, in most instances, the physical center of the plant could serve as an adequate operational aiming point. Nevertheless, the aiming-point reports gave precision to EOU thinking on target problems and added a new element to the general stream of target intelligence work. It should, perhaps, be underlined that the American strategic bombing effort and operations in support of D-Day were based overwhelmingly on British intelligence, whose officers threw themselves into support of American operations in a memorable and wholehearted way not merely to carry forward a war against a common enemy but also, to a degree, because precision bombing brought into play more of the information they had accumulated and the remarkable skills they had developed than did area bombing.

As the laborious aiming-point reports were pressed forward, EOU was drawn, starting in December 1942, into the formulation of its own concepts of target-system selection. Appendix B includes four memoranda which, among them, provide a fair picture of how EOU came to think about target selection, including its view of area bombing.

Briefly, we sought target systems where the destruction of the minimum number of targets would have the greatest, most prompt, and most long-lasting direct military effect. Each of the modifiers carried weight. One had to ask, in assessing the results of an attack, how large its effect would be within its own sector of the economy or military system; how quickly would the effect be felt; how long would it last; and what its direct military (as opposed to economic) consequences would be. The application of these criteria was serious and rather rigorous intellectual business. It required, among other things, taking fully into account the extent to which the military effect of an attack could be cushioned by the Germans, notably, by diverting civilian output or services to military purposes or buying time for repair by drawing down stocks of finished products or in the pipeline. In all this our knowledge as economists of the structure of production, buttressed by what we had learned from the logistical studies in Washington and aiming-point reports, converged with the military principles of Hughes, Anderson, and the British Air Staff. But there was something of the Austrian theory of capital and Leontieff's input-output matrix in our way of looking at things.

The EOU view was, then, both a theory of bombing policy

and a related method of analysis. It insisted that targets be chosen in the light of an explicitly defined military aim, linked to the full context of war strategy and, especially, to its timing. It opposed attacks designed simply to weaken the German economy in some generalized sense or to cause political disruption, and it emphasized the possibilities of evading the military consequences of bomb damage in a mature and resourceful economic system like that of wartime Germany. (We would have emphasized the latter point still more strongly if we had known at the time how far short of full economic mobilization Germany was down to the spring of 1944.) EOU doctrine insisted on the need to concentrate bombing attacks against the minimum number of targets whose destruction would achieve the specified military goal and on the need for perseverance and thoroughness when the attack on a target system had been launched. The EOU view was, in short, a doctrine of warfare, not of economics or politics.

In elaborating this doctrine in particular contexts, EOU's contribution had a distinguishing characteristic: it was an intelligence organization at the working level. It was, in fact, the only organization in the European theater devoted solely to the development of target intelligence and target thinking. It was a continuing rule of the unit that its personnel remain close to the basic raw information; and its papers, even at their most theoretical, stood against a background of research: the steady reading of the flow of ground reports, the building-by-building analysis of the targets themselves, the measurement of the bridges, the cleaning and recording of markings from a pile of German ball bearings. These grubby exercises were never far from the surface of thought. The unit was sufficiently large to handle the full flow of intelligence and sufficiently small and flexible so that the major items in each field were shared. Long-term specialization was not encouraged. At one time or another most members of the unit were reigning experts on aircraft, ball bearings, and oil.

4. The Winning of Daylight Air Supremacy over Germany

By early 1943 our common grasp on what we regarded as the correct principles of target selection for precision bombing outranged the capabilities of the Eighth Air Force. As it slowly built up its strength, it confronted the realities of European weather, Germany's powerful anti-aircraft batteries, and the German daylight single-engine fighter force, well equipped and expertly manned.

On June 10, 1943, Portal, working closely with the Eighth Air Force, narrowed the spacious set of target systems in the Casablanca directive of January 21, 1943, to German submarine construction yards, the aircraft industry, and plants producing ball bearings. The German transport system and oil production were dropped from the Casablanca directive as beyond the existing capacity of the Eighth Air Force. The combined bomber offensive implementing Portal's instruction was code-named POINTBLANK. EOU was an active participant in its formulation and execution.

But execution was by no means easy. Just when RAF Bomber Command was demonstrating a capacity to do considerable damage to German cities, the Eighth Air Force was finding it exceedingly difficult to penetrate deeply into Germany to strike significant targets. The targets that most urgently needed hitting were the factories producing German fighter aircraft. In 1943 a massive expansion in production and first-line strength was under way. The acceptance of single-engine fighter aircraft into the German air force almost tripled between January and July 1943. Strength in units rose proportionately. The figures were expected to double by the end of the year. Production remained concentrated at well-known plants whose expanding contours were watched with anxious fascination in aerial photographs. The Germans did not believe they were subject to massive precision attack.

British pressure on the Eighth Air Force to join the RAF in nighttime area bombing was resisted at high and low levels while the American air forces struggled to create the conditions which would make their commitment to daylight precision bombing effective. The development of the long-range fighter was accelerated; the bomber's defensive capabilities were strengthened by chin turrets, tighter formations, and other devices; area bombing in daylight with radar was introduced to permit bad weather days over target areas to be used; and methods for dealing with poor weather conditions on takeoff were devised. But only time could bring the buildup of the long-range fighters which were needed if Germany was to be effectively attacked by daylight, and the superiority of American long-range fighters over German short-range fighters could by no means be guaranteed in advance. Out of the experience of the Battle of Britain many in London believed short-range fighters would always command a substantial inherent advantage over pilots and planes that had to come to the scene of battle over long distances.

The Army Air Forces thus faced in mid-1943 a most painful choice: the choice of postponing by perhaps six months (until long-range fighters were available on a large scale) the precision attack on objectives in Germany, while the German fighter defense forces doubled, or of attacking German targets without long-range fighter support, with high losses.

The American air forces decided that, despite its evident limitations and the promise of more bombers and long-range fighters by early 1944, it would proceed immediately with precision bombing attacks deep in Germany. More than any other man, Fred Anderson was responsible for that decision—although many, both in the United States and in Europe, shared in shaping and executing it.

The modern U.S. Air Force as a fighting establishment—rather than a small body of dedicated pilots, production plans, and untested convictions—emerged directly from the crisis imposed by the need to make this choice, a crisis which can be dated from July to December 1943. A generation of leaders, a firm operational doctrine, a set of mature staff concepts, and a fighting style crystalized over these decisive months. The character of the modern U.S. Air Force cannot be understood outside the context of that experience.

Between July and December 1943 some sixteen attacks were delivered against the German aircraft and antifriction bearing industries. These were mainly mounted from Britain, but a few were carried out by the Fifteenth Air Force, which was primarily engaged in support of ground-force operations in the Mediterranean theater. Forty-six hundred tons of bombs were dropped on aircraft factories in these crucial six months: a mere 4 percent of the total American effort during this period, about one-third of 1 percent of the total bombing effort of the American air forces in the Second World War in Europe. These few attacks were, however, of immense importance. German single-engine fighter production, which had risen from less than 400 in January 1943 to 1,050 in July, was down to less than 600 by December, a decline caused by direct bomb damage combined with the effects of dispersal induced by the fear of further damage. In the absence of bombing attacks, the figure by December might well have been on the order of 2,000 per month. Table 1 lists the monthly figures for 1943.

Beyond the loss of about three months' output of German fighter aircraft, the unexpected success of these few gallant, costly missions led the Germans to disperse their production at a crucial stage of the war. This dispersal was conducted with energy and success, but its timing was disastrous to

TABLE 1. German Single-Engine Fighter Aircraft Acceptances, 1943

January	381	July	1,050
February	725	August	914
March	819	September	853
April	790	October	955
May	847	November	775
June	957	December	560

Source: U.S. Strategic Bombing Survey, Overall Economic Effects Division, "The Effects of Strategic Bombing on the German War Economy," October 31, 1945, p. 156.

German interests. Just when German fighter production was beginning to recover from the 1943 attacks, the Army Air Forces made their bid for daylight air supremacy over Germany, backed at last by an effective long-range fighter, the P-51, available in quantity. A limited break in the winter weather occurred on January 11, and several attacks on aircraft plants were carried out. The major result, however, was the demonstration that the long-range fighters could deal successfully with the German defensive fighter force. Then came the Big Week.

Exploiting a remarkable sequence of clear days in the European winter, the American air forces at last executed Portal's directive of June 10, 1943. They attacked the aircraft and bearing industries of Germany in great force on February 20–25, 1944, following a plan which had been developed and held in readiness for many months. On the night of February 19 the attack was ordered on the assumption that it might cost one hundred or more American bombers and their crews. Spaatz made this extremely difficult command decision knowing that either the Americans had to act on their air force concepts, and take their losses, or admit they had been wrong. And he was fully aware of the repercussions on the Army Air Forces of the loss of sixty bombers in a single raid in October 1943. The losses on February 20 were only twenty-two. And, following fundamental military principle, the breakthrough was driven home day after day, despite the strain on the crews (and the understandable resistance of their commanders), until normal winter weather again closed in on February 26.

Substantial damage was done to German aircraft and ball-bearing production, and the Germans were forced into accelerated dispersal. But this was a military victory for the American air forces, not a victory over German production capabilities. The attack of February 1944 was important because the German fighter force was tactically defeated in the air in close and bitter battle, and it never again recovered major capabilities for sustained defensive operations in daylight. This tactical defeat took the form of the progressive loss of experienced pilots at a greater rate than in the American fighter force; and, partly due to later attacks on oil and their effects on pilot training, this loss could never again be made good by the Germans.

Adolf Galland, wartime commander of the German fighter forces, captures vividly the sequence in which this critical process occurred:

> In December, 1943, the P-51 Mustang was introduced into the Eighth AAF, the technical details of which we had known already for some time. In the beginning of 1944 it was used more and more frequently and finally took over the task of escorting the American bomber units, while the P-47 Thunderbolt at first gave additional fighter protection and later operated mainly as a fighter-bomber.
>
> The German destroyer, which so far had achieved good results in the fight against the multiengined bombers, now suffered unbearable losses because of the American fighter escort. The fighters that accompanied the destroyers were soon involved in dogfights with the numerically superior enemy, so that they were fully occupied themselves and the destroyers had to fend for themselves. . . .
>
> . . . With the increasing strength of the Mustang fighter

escort we also lost more of our fighters. Therefore we used the tactic of combat formations. The destroyers and heavily armed fighters assembled in the same area with numerous light groups of fighters. They attacked together.

A combat formation usually consisted of one attacking group and two escort groups. The former were to attack the enemy's bomber formation while the latter gave them fighter protection against the enemy fighters which were numerically many times stronger. These combat formations were an emergency measure forced on us by the enemy and it was anything but ideal. Anyhow they fulfilled the demand for concentration of forces up to the maximum which I always postulated. But other shortcomings soon appeared. The combat formations had become unwieldy forms, needing much more time for assembly and for climbing to the required altitude for the action than the single groups of fighters. But what was worse, the introduction of this tactic meant renouncing the fundamental principle of fighter action: at all times and in all places to be offensive. According to orders the combat formations were not to attack the American fighter escort, thus losing the initiative and making it easier for the enemy to take the decisive step from the defensive, which was their escorting duty, to the offensive. The results were devastating, because only the fighter that attacks has the advantage. Our losses rose irresistibly. Forced onto the defensive our units forgot how to conduct a dogfight. Now it had come to banking and diving away. Naturally any cohesion of the unit was lost, and singly our fighters were finished off by the enemy who outnumbered them greatly.

This development was undoubtedly catastrophic and it started with the order to attack the bombers only. This stage at which the German fighter arm had arrived represented only a link in a chain of disastrous mistakes. Only in this way can it be explained that the great struggle for air supremacy over Germany between the opposing fighters never took place.

In April, 1944, I said in one of my reports: "The ratio in

> which we fight today is about 1 to 7. The standard of the Americans is extraordinarily high. The day fighters have lost more than 1000 aircraft during the last four months, among them our best officers. These gaps cannot be filled. During each enemy raid we lose about 50 fighters. Things have gone so far that the danger of a collapse of our arm exists."[15]

Thus the strategic attacks on fighter production in 1943 may well have succeeded in containing the German fighter force at a size which permitted the close tactical victory of February 1944. Precision bombing was the instrument and the occasion by which the equivalent of the Battle of Britain was won by the air forces over Germany; but the formal victory was tactical and took the form of a subsequent supremacy of American fighter aircraft, which permitted freedom to the daylight bombers at acceptable cost. American bomber forces continued to suffer losses, sometimes heavy losses; but never again was their ability to sustain significant operations throughout Europe in question. The indispensable foundation for OVERLORD was at last established. Webster and Frankland quite properly entitle the chapter introducing this turn of events ". . . the Revival of U.S. Strategic Power."

5. The Choice of Oil and Its Initial Defeat

An awareness of the transition of the American strategic bombers from trivial capabilities in the autumn of 1942 to virtual dominance in daylight over Germany by the end of February 1944 is necessary for an understanding of the debate leading up to Eisenhower's decision of March 25 and the debates which followed. As the Big Week (February 20–25) unfolded successfully, Hughes and EOU went to work on the optimum method for exploiting the breakthrough.

In retrospect, the choice of oil was an obvious next step. It promised, if sedulously pursued, not only to affect the whole German war production structure but also to limit the fighting capacity of the ground and air forces. With D-Day only three months off, this was a decisive consideration. The oil industry was so located as to offer an excellent distribution of targets, and, especially, it offered scope for the growing capabilities of the purposeful and efficient Fifteenth Air Force. Although large by older standards, it was a sufficiently limited target system to offer a chance of cutting deep within a reasonably short period of time and to leave some effort for containing the aircraft and ball-bearing target systems and for striking at such attractive concentrations as tank engine production.

The choice of oil as the major next step was agreed on by EOU and the Air Forces planners before the week of consecutive attacks on the aircraft industry had ended; and EOU's suggested draft of the plan, "The Use of Strategic Air Power after 1 March 1944," was finished on February 28. The draft reviewed the history of the existing bombing directive; evaluated the position of the target systems under attack; and explored the merits of oil and the more likely alternatives to oil, including the systematic attack on rail transport centers. It included a number of detailed appendixes. This paper was sent to Hughes who, with Pearré Cabell, recently drawn into planning from operational command, was charged with the preparation of the USSTAF plan. The final version used the EOU appendixes in their entirety, and the text drew heavily on the EOU draft. I was allocated to help in the preparation of the plan in final form, while Kindleberger hurriedly rounded up, from the various oil pundits, testimonials to the probable efficacy of the proposed oil attacks. These were judged to be useful, for the previous history of attacks on oil had, on the whole, been one of disappointment, and all possible reinforcements were thought necessary.

On the evening of March 5, 1944, Cabell and Hughes presented the final draft to General Spaatz. Anderson had already read the plan and was an advocate of it. Discussion began before dinner and ran into the early hours of the morning around the conference table at Spaatz' headquarters. Despite the effort to emphasize, within the plan, the will to complete the attacks on the POINTBLANK systems, General Spaatz quickly appreciated that it was to all intents and purposes an oil plan. He explored at length the issues at stake, especially the capabilities of the Eighth and Fifteenth Air Forces with respect to the number of targets involved. He then ordered the plan completed for prompt presentation to Portal and Eisenhower. Anderson, Cabell, Hughes, and I waited around Spaatz' headquarters while the staff reproduced the final version of the plan, playing Ping-Pong and otherwise celebrating the arrival of a message from Washington announcing Cabell's elevation to general officer rank. Kindleberger appeared in the morning with the requisite oil testimonials and took over from me.

A critical part of EOU's analysis related to the estimated level of German oil stocks and rates of oil consumption. These variables would determine, along with damage actually inflicted on German oil production and minimum necessary allocation to the German economy, the timing of the effect on German military operations of the proposed oil offensive. As the following passage notes, these estimates were the product of collective efforts within the Anglo-American intelligence community.

> *Production and Stocks.* If refineries and synthetic plants are not attacked, it is estimated that Axis production of liquid fuels and lubricants during the six months following 1 March 1944 will be 8.6 million tons, comprised as follows:
>
> | | |
> |---|---|
> | Crude and shale oil products | 4.1 million tons |
> | Synthetic oil products | 3.3 " " |
> | Substitutes, vegetable oils, etc. | 1.2 " " |
>
> Estimated stocks of finished products as of 1 March 1944 are about four million tons, equivalent to about three months' output and consumption. These stocks include reserves and the entire distributional pipeline, approximately as follows:
>
> | | |
> |---|---|
> | Military and civil reserves | 1.0 million tons |
> | Operating stocks at consumption points | 1.6 " " |
> | Stocks in transit | .6 " " |
> | Stocks at refineries and synthetic plants | .8 " " |
> | | 4.0 " " |

Note: Figures on output, consumption, and stocks are taken or interpolated from papers by U.S. Enemy Oil Committee and British Hartley Committee.

Not all of these stocks could be consumed by the military if output ceased. Some of the stocks at refineries and synthetic plants would be destroyed in bombing. And some of the reserves, operating stocks, and in transit stocks would not be the particular type of products needed (e.g., industrial fuel oil would not satisfy a need for petrol or lubricants).

These figures were the basis for the following conclusion:

> ... no other target system holds such great promise for hastening German defeat. Stocks of finished petroleum products are sufficient only for several months' military operations. The loss of more than 50% of Axis output would directly and materially reduce German military capabilities through reducing tactical and strategic mobility and front-line delivery of supplies. It would indirectly affect military capabilities through weakening High Command morale and industrial ability to produce weapons and supplies.
>
> The extension of attacks to storage facilities in Western Europe might directly impair German mobility in deploying to meet Overlord. Indirect benefit to Overlord would, in any case, result from the lessened mobility of German divisions in Finland and Norway, Russia, the Balkans and Italy.

This paper, rooted in the work not only of EOU but of the Anglo-American intelligence community as a whole, was the basis for the interventions on oil by Spaatz, Anderson, and Lawrence (of MEW) on March 25. The critical weakness of the argument is suggested in the quite different statements on the timing of the effects of the attack on oil (see Appendix A):

— "*Spaatz*: ... the execution of the oil plan would force the enemy to decide to reduce oil consumption in anticipation of an impending shortage and consequent reduction in fighting power."

— "*Anderson*: ... although U.S.ST.A.F. could not guarantee that the attacks of oil targets would have an appreciable effect during the initial stages of OVERLORD their studies showed that the Transportation Plan would also not have such an

effect. On the other hand, the oil plan would have a decisive effect within a period of about six months whereas they did not think that the Transportation Plan would have a decisive effect within any measurable length of time."

— "*Lawrence*: . . . it had been calculated that if U.S.ST.A.F. completed their plan of attacking 27 oil installations within a period of three months then by the time a further three months was up the Germans would have had to institute a cut of 25% in their present military consumption. (This was assuming that they still hold the Roumanian oilfields.) What we could not estimate was how they would distribute this cut as between the various fronts. It was thought that they had large stocks in the West so that the effect need not be immediate. He [Lawrence] thought that there would certainly be some effect noticeable in the West four or five months after the plan began to be put into effect."

These ambiguities about timing permitted Portal to conclude—paraphrasing Lawrence and Anderson, rather than Spaatz—in a way that virtually settled the matter in Tedder's favor: ". . . this showed conclusively that the oil plan would not help OVERLORD in the first few critical weeks. It was, rather, a longer term plan which might have greater overall effects on the course of the war as a whole than the transportation plan but it would be six months before these were felt appreciably. He agreed however that the oil plan had great attractions and he thought we should seriously consider adopting it after the first crisis of OVERLORD was passed and we were firmly established on the Continent."

While EOU's contribution on oil was fairly represented at the March 25 meeting, its views on tactical targets were not.

6. EOU Goes Tactical

As 1943 drew to a close it was apparent that a new stage in the planning of the invasion was imminent. Kindleberger suggested several times to Hughes that EOU might urgently interest itself in tactical target problems, but only speculative general discussion resulted.

In January the Theater Intelligence Section of G-2, SHAEF, issued a paper suggesting various particular transport and army establishment targets which might usefully be attacked before D-Day in support of the invasion. This document, while attempting soberly to relate air operations to the ground-force problem of invasion, was clearly inadequate. This was the paper to which Zuckerman reacted negatively and which was swept aside and superseded in AEAF by his January 22 memorandum, "Delay and Disorganization of Enemy Movement by Rail," calling for an attack on the marshalling yards of France and Belgium on a very large scale, analogous to the attack on the Sicilian and Italian marshalling yards in the summer of 1943 (see above, pp. 12–13).

Zuckerman's paper was sent to USSTAF; Hughes invited EOU's view. The AEAF plan crystalized the thinking and energies of the unit very quickly indeed. A brief reply was passed to Colonel Hughes on January 27, and a more detailed reply on February 7.

EOU saw serious reasons for disagreement in the outlook implicit in the Zuckerman paper and the specific line of argument advanced. In terms of the targeting principles that EOU had evolved, Zuckerman's plan had two basic weaknesses. The effects of bombing marshalling yards on the German capacity to bring troops and supplies by rail to the front would be diluted by:

1. The vast excess capacity that marshalling yards represented, since they were constructed for the efficient manipulation of civilian rail traffic; only a single through line was required to move military traffic through a bombed marshalling yard.

2. The exceedingly short time required to repair bombed tracks.

More broadly, EOU's reaction—and that of Hughes, Anderson, and Spaatz—was roughly this, notably after the Big Week in February. After a desperately close struggle over the previous months, the U.S. strategic air forces had finally achieved a capability to bomb with reasonable precision in daylight virtually any target in Germany with modest losses. The victory over the German daylight fighter forces was, essentially, a defensive victory. It was a necessary condition for OVERLORD and a necessary condition for the positive application of strategic air power. As of the end of February, the time had arrived for that positive use of air power. The tactical breakthrough represented by daylight air supremacy should be exploited to the full by attacking the targets in Germany whose destruction had the maximum chance of significantly shortening the war. And oil was clearly the optimum target system. Only a few believed—or still hoped —that the war could be won by the use of air power alone, without the invasion of the Continent. The Army Air Forces had to do everything in their power to contribute to the success of the invasion. But they were in a position to do more: to weaken gravely the enemy's capacity to resist on land and in the air, on every front. But at just this moment Spaatz was confronted by a plan which risked permitting the Luftwaffe to recover its capacity to defend Germany in daylight and to obstruct the Normandy invasion, which would deny the American bomber force the possibility of attacking oil and which represented a dubious and second-rate method for using air power in direct support of the Allied landings and subsequent ground-force operations.

Tedder and Zuckerman did not share the vicissitudes of daylight precision bombing of 1942–1943. Their minds were controlled by what were, no doubt, equally memorable experiences in the Mediterranean and the concepts generated by them. But their memoirs do not reflect awareness of the impact on the Americans (and a good many British) of the Big Week in February when daylight air supremacy was won. They appear to have taken it for granted. They were, after all, focused on how to translate the concepts they had developed in the Mediterranean into policy in Western Europe. This difference in experience and perspective contributed something to the intensity of the clash which occurred.

It was obvious to EOU, however, that an expression of its frustrations was not sufficient. A better plan in support of D-Day would be necessary; and some of the AEAF allegations about experience in the Mediterranean, the capabilities of the air force against bridges, and the structure and resilience of the European rail system would have to be met. Carl Kaysen was hurriedly recalled from damage-assessment work at Princes Risborough, and plans were made to enlarge the EOU staff to meet its largely self-imposed commitments in the new field.

After canvassing current opinion in the Mediterranean and consulting various persons in London who had experience with transport problems and bombing policy generally, there seemed to be grounds for optimism. First, it appeared that the Sicilian experience was open to serious question as a justification for the attack on marshalling yards, and that tactical-target thinking in the Mediterranean over the winter of 1943–1944 had moved away from the conception of attack on the whole railway system toward systematic attacks on bridges and lines over some distance behind the front. At the moment when the voice of Mediterranean experience was being invoked in London by Tedder and Zuckerman in support of marshalling yards, the air forces in Italy were completing successfully their first full experiment with Operation STRANGLE, a systematic interdiction effort north of Rome, having relegated the attack on marshalling yards in northern Italy to secondary priority (see below, pp. 57–58).

It also became clear that, on grounds similar to those held by EOU, the AEAF plan was not supported by Air Ministry and War Office experts, or by Lawrence, the senior target analyst at MEW.

This situation led to the production of some hopeful EOU papers. They included a massive analysis of the Zuckerman paper on the marshalling-yard attacks in Sicily, whose conclusions are suggested in the following summary passage, dated February 22, 1944:

> 1. Professor Zuckerman's evaluation of air attacks on transport facilities in the Mediterranean during the first half of 1943 concludes that they achieved profound strategic results, despite their tactical failure, because of the widespread destruction of Sicilian and Southern Italian rolling-stock and locomotive repair facilities, damaged in heavy attacks on marshalling yards. It also concludes that the interdiction of communication which might be produced by the blocking of rail lines at bridges, junctions, and open line is uneconomical.
> 2. The present paper concludes, on the basis of the evidence in Professor Zuckerman's paper, that the principal factor contributing to the 300,000 ton reduction in Sicilian imports during the first half of 1943 was the gradual reduction in ferrying capacity across the Messina Straits, which was only slightly influenced by marshalling-yard attacks. It is believed that the reduction in Sicilian railroad traffic was the result and not the cause of this decline in imports; and it is believed that the figures for serviceable locomotives and the fact that rolling-stock was returned to the mainland empty

suggest strongly that damage to these was irrelevant to the results.

3. More recent evidence is presented to show that the direct interdiction of communication at bridges and lines is cheaper in terms of effort and of greater duration than blocks to marshalling yards.

4. Finally, it is argued that the distinction between a strategic success and a tactical failure is meaningless when applied to a circumscribed theatre of operation.

A further commentary, in the form of a memorandum to Hughes, had deployed specific information from the Mediterranean (dated February 8, 1944):

1. Several days ago we cabled our OSS officer in Italy, engaged in the selection of tactical targets for paratroops, airborne infantry and other ground attack units, for comment on the statement that the Germans' southernmost railhead during the latter part of the Sicilian campaign was north of Naples, this being due to the devastating attacks on the southern Italian marshalling yards. His reply has just been received; the following paragraphs present the substance of the reply.

2. The record indicates that the Germans were not south of Salerno, after the campaign in Sicily, in sufficient force to involve any major supply problems. The major contributing factors to the Germans' withdrawal from Southern Italy in September and the use of northern railheads were the slight size of the force and the prospect and actuality of the Salerno landings on 3rd September 1943. The bombing of the yards at Foggia, Naples, and Battipalgia was effective in buttressing the German decision not to try to stay in Southern Italy, but was less important than the threat of encirclement landings and the lack of Italian will to resist our landings.

3. The fact that the Germans are still in Rome, despite the major portions of a considerable transport bombing effort being directed against marshalling yards since the beginning of the year, is testimony of the ineffectiveness of this type of

attack. Data are being assembled and will be forwarded shortly.

4. A study of damage reports from October to January indicates that bridge attacks were more effective in producing actual cuts in line than attacks against yards. Overlooking the very important fact that cuts in line in marshalling yards can be easily repaired while bridges cannot, a bridge blockage required 196 tons while the stoppage of traffic through a yard required 456 tons of bombs. It is obvious that the last track in a yard is no wider than the last track on a bridge, despite the large overall size of marshalling yards.

5. The fact that yard attacks delay some traffic is immaterial since the impact of delay falls upon less important traffic; military supplies, a very small proportion of total traffic, are not delayed. Yard attacks might help if line blockage was not possible, but only if the vast cushion of excess capacity could be kept below the point where yard capacity was insufficient to handle direct military traffic. Also, in the event that blockage of lines took place, yard attacks in the specific instance in which it is known that military traffic is piled up and congested may be useful.

6. It is my strong recommendation that the feasibility of low level cratering of long stretches of open country line be considered.[16]

From mid-February onward EOU, reinforced with Bob Roosa, plunged into the development of a positive alternative to the marshalling-yard plan. Briefly, it was agreed that the optimum pre–D-Day tactical program should consist in:

1. Attack on target systems of bridges, junctions, and open stretches of rail line designed to deny the enemy through rail access to the bridgehead area.

2. Attack on ammunition and fuel dumps, ordnance depots, and other military establishments on which the German defense in the West would depend, offering concentrations suitable to bombing attack.

In all its many subsequent versions, these were the two

continuing strands in EOU's tactical proposals. It was felt that such a program was superior because it would accomplish the disruption of military-supply movements by rail more thoroughly than the attack on marshalling yards; and it would do so at much less cost in effort. As a result, heavy bomber effort would be available to begin immediately the strategic attack on oil and to exploit the considerable concentrations of military resources which the Germans had permitted to persist within their western military establishment, in the form of fuel, ammunition, and ordnance dumps. Although it was not an overriding criterion, we took some comfort that our proposals would be much less costly in terms of the lives of civilians than would the marshalling-yard attacks.

To move from the conception of this program to adequate target priority lists required a very considerable mobilization of the intelligence. A large proportion of EOU effort was devoted to this project over subsequent weeks. Within the War Office, G-2 SHAEF, and other files, the bulk of the necessary raw material existed, in one form or another. Under Kindleberger's direction, Harold Barnett, Kaysen, Roosa, and Mark Kahn set out to collect, evaluate, and order it and to emerge with meaningful physical targets. In one way or another the basic data were collected; by the end of March the Seine and Loire bridges—and two further, more distant rings of bridges—had been fully analyzed,[17] as well as a large number of the more important dumps, headquarters, and other tactical targets directly related to front-line military capabilities.

By February 17—even before detailed staff work had been completed—an "Outline Plan for Air Support of Overlord" was written by EOU incorporating the bridge and military-supplies program. This was submitted to USSTAF, but no immediate action was taken. When Kindleberger and I were called in to help in the formulation of the oil program, early in March, we urged USSTAF to support explicitly, within the new strategic plan, a tactical plan in opposition to that of AEAF, since the latter had not yet been formally adopted by

Eisenhower. Spaatz decided, however, that the case for oil would be put forward separately.

Thus, on March 25 Eisenhower was presented with false alternatives: marshalling yards versus oil. The true alternatives were oil, plus a sustained systematic attack on bridges and dumps, versus marshalling yards. The record does not reveal whether Eisenhower was aware that a detailed, fully staffed alternative tactical plan in support of the landings existed;[18] but the reasons which led Spaatz not to lay a tactical plan before Eisenhower and Portal on March 25 are tolerably clear, and they take us into the arena of power, vested interest, and personality where forces quite different from straightforward intellectual argument were at work.

7. The Arena of Decision: Power, Vested Interest, and Personality

Spaatz chose not to present the case for bridges and dumps versus marshalling yards for two reasons. First, he was in command of a strategic, not a tactical, air force. He was prepared to argue that the bombing of oil would have tactical effects, that the attacks on oil would keep the German fighter force in Germany and impose on it the heavy attrition needed to reduce its tactical capabilities for D-Day, and that the marshalling-yards plan would risk permitting a revival of German fighter strength. But he was not prepared to argue—at least not in the formal showdown of March 25—for a tactical plan involving the use of the tactical bombers assigned to other commanders, as well as the Eighth and Fifteenth Air Forces.

This rather strict military correctness was reinforced by a second consideration. The American air commanders (like a great many of the British military) were by no means sure that the landings in Normandy would succeed. Spaatz, in particular, had grave doubts about the viability of the exercise. If it failed, he believed the U.S. Army Air Forces would be called upon, along with the RAF, to try to win the war by the maximum application of air power. But, should the landings fail, Spaatz was determined the record would show that he had done everything Eisenhower had asked him to do. As Hughes' memoir says: "At this tense juncture, the intellectual niceties of planning were far from his [Spaatz'] mind. If Eisenhower had asked him, in writing, to drop his bombs in the Arctic Ocean on D-Day he would have complied." Responding to an earlier draft of this book, Kaysen recalled a particular occasion when Spaatz turned down the suggestion that he formally advocate an independent tactical plan:

> I attended a meeting in Spaatz' office at Widewing about a week or ten days before the great show-down [March 25] in the capacity of invisible man as Cabell's bag carrier. Others present in addition to Cabell and Spaatz were F. L. Anderson and Orvil Anderson. . . . Cabell . . . was the spokesman for our plan. After Cabell presented it, F. L. Anderson spoke for it, partly on the ground that the marshalling-yard plan would have assigned 8th AF the task of bombing French and Belgian railway centers in daylight. Thus "we," rather than the RAF, attacking by night, would get the blame for killing French and Belgian civilians. (I believe this point was later raised by Spaatz with the Combined Chiefs.)
>
> After listening, Spaatz clapped his battered Air-Corps style cap on his head, rose from his desk, paced the room, and delivered himself of the following (more or less): "I won't do it. I won't take the responsibility. This ——— ——— invasion can't succeed, and I don't want any part of the blame. After it fails, we can show them how we can win by bombing."

There was undoubtedly more to it than that. Like everyone else, Spaatz passionately wanted the landings to succeed. Moreover, he had been with Eisenhower and Tedder through the difficult Mediterranean campaign. He understood the importance of harnessing ground, naval, and air power into a team; and, by instinct and temperament, he was a team man as well as a dedicated Air Force officer. His ties to Eisenhower went back to West Point where they were contemporaries, Spaatz being one class ahead. Although Spaatz regarded the proposed transport plan as a second-rate method for supporting the invasion force in the critical early days, he would not have felt comfortable—in human as well as hierarchical terms—challenging Tedder directly with a tactical plan of his own in the field of responsibility that Tedder had been assigned, gravely embarrassing Eisenhower in the bargain.

Tedder, too, had several problems that transcended optimum targeting. He arrived in January 1944, as Eisenhower's deputy, with special responsibilities for the use of air power in support of the invasion, to find Harris and, from Tedder's perspective, Spaatz, as well, determined to pursue their respective attacks on Germany. He needed a plan which would bring the strategic as well as tactical bombers to bear on his and Eisenhower's problem and under their command. Specifically, he was confronted with a proposal to put bombing policy under several committees, to which he reacted strongly to Portal on February 22: "I do not think that a unified plan can be evolved by a number of independent committees, and I am quite certain that successful operations cannot result from control by committees."[19] In conferences with Spaatz and Harris, Tedder found agreement that in the weeks immediately before and after D-Day they were prepared to concentrate their forces on tactical targets. Tedder argued: "that paralysis of the French railway system could not be achieved in a week or two. Unless we did the job properly, there would be little advantage in trying to do it at all; and if we did decide on the Transportation Plan, it must be carried out with our full resources. Even though the alternative was heavy damage to the German synthetic oil plants, that could not vitally affect the enemy's efforts in time for 'Overlord.'"[20] Evidently, the question of timing and targets related also to the question of who would exercise control over the strategic bombers and for how long.

Tedder's problem was complicated by the awkward and ambiguous position of Leigh-Mallory. Nominally, the latter was in charge of the air effort in support of the invasion and responsible for producing a plan. That is why Zuckerman was assigned to the AEAF. But Leigh-Mallory did not command the respect of Churchill, Harris, or Spaatz. The latter simply refused to place his force under Leigh-Mallory's orders. Eisenhower had wanted Tedder as his air commander, as in the Mediterranean. At British insistence he accepted him as his over-all deputy. In retrospect, it is difficult to understand why the British permitted Leigh-Mallory to be placed in such a sensitive position in the chain of command unless it was envisaged from the beginning that he would receive his orders from Tedder; but for a time, at least, his role complicated Tedder's and everyone else's task.

Quite aside from Tedder's honest assessment of what the optimum targeting plan should be, it is clear that the marshalling-yard plan appealed to Tedder as a way of solving the problem of command. Here was a program requiring the concentration of all bomber forces, for a protracted period, under centralized command. And, certainly, there was an understandable element of personal pride in all this: "The new plan, based on my Mediterranean experience, was to paralyse the railways by systematic attack on railway centres, and came to be known as the Transportation Plan. This plan was to run like a thread through all the operations up to the end of the war; true, sometimes a very tangled thread —tangled sometimes by deliberate intrigue and sometimes by ignorance and misunderstanding."[21]

As Tedder's evocation of "intrigue," "ignorance," and "misunderstanding" suggests, he found it difficult or impossible to believe that the lessons of his Mediterranean experience were open to legitimate debate or that, quite aside from the Mediterranean experience, knowledgeable men could believe that his transport plan was not sufficient to prevent the Germans from bringing military forces and supplies forward to the Channel by rail. It is unclear whether he was aware of a fully developed bridge-and-dump alternative. Almost certainly he was. But he was clearly not in a mood to lay it before Eisenhower on March 25. Marshalling yards versus oil presented much more comfortable terms for debate. Tedder significantly referred to all alternative tactical plans as requiring coordinated attacks for a short period straddling D-Day. This was not the case, for the bridge-and-dump plan (excepting the Loire bridges) could have been conducted over a protracted period without compromising the area chosen for the invasion landing. As we shall see, the bridge plan was, in fact, launched a month before D-Day and could well have been initiated earlier, to good effect.

Eisenhower's central problem in all this, as he saw it, was still more remote from the question of optimum targeting. He was determined—and understandably determined—that in assuming responsibility for the success of the invasion he should have at his disposal all the resources available in his theater, including the strategic bombers. This involved not only the question of bringing Harris and Spaatz into line but also his authority vis-à-vis the Combined Chiefs of Staff and the British government. The British cabinet was determined to maintain independence for Coastal Command and also to be able to call on the bombers for attacks on the launching sites for flying bombs—a program called CROSSBOW. The details of this tangled tale are well documented in the official histories, but its importance to Eisenhower is worth underlining. In a memorandum for the record of March 22, 1944, reviewing his first three months of command, Eisenhower identified the issue as one of his major problems and reviewed it in these terms:

> The air problem has been one requiring a great deal of patience and negotiation. I found, upon coming here, that the British had a great fear that the American idea was to seize all the air in Great Britain and apply it very locally in the preparation of OVERLORD. It took long and patient explaining to show ———
> a. That we had no great interest in Coastal Command, which organization would have to continue in its present set-up, although it would be most useful in protecting our ships as we went into the assault;
> b. that a discontinuance of POINTBLANK was furthest

from our minds because through POINTBLANK is about our only means of forcing the German Air Force to fight, and thus allow us to gain ascendancy over it;

c. that the big bomber, particularly the Command Bombing Force, was not to be misused on targets for which it is not particularly suited.

After long discussions and negotiation it developed that the British did not trust Leigh-Mallory to be the directing head of my Air Forces. This came as somewhat of a surprise to me since I understood he had been especially selected by the British themselves for this post. I found, on the other hand, that they did trust Tedder and I immediately announced, through written memorandum, that Tedder would be the directing head of all my Air Forces, with Leigh-Mallory, Spaatz and Harris operating on a coordinate plane. I definitely proposed that the turning over of Spaatz' and Harris' Air Forces to me should be made consequent upon the approval by Portal and myself of a general air preparation plan which would take into account all of the objectives of POINTBLANK so far as they were consistent with our great need for preparing for OVERLORD. In the messages coming back and forth from Washington a sudden argument developed between [sic] the use of the word "command." This whole matter I had considered settled a week ago, after many weeks of argument. This did not seem important at the time the drafts were first drawn up, but as long as the question was raised I have recommended to General Marshall that a word be adopted that leaves no doubt in anybody's mind of my authority and responsibility for controlling air operations of all three of these Forces during the critical period of OVERLORD.

The actual air preparatory plan is to be the subject of a formal meeting on this coming Saturday, March 25, between Portal, Spaatz, Harris, Leigh-Mallory, Tedder and myself.

If a satisfactory answer is not reached I am going to take drastic action and inform the Combined Chiefs of Staff that unless the matter is settled at once I will request relief from this Command.[22]

In asserting his authority successfully, however, Eisenhower was clearly sensitive to the complex of differing interests in play. Given all the circumstances surrounding Tedder's appointment, and his status as the highest-ranking British figure in OVERLORD, his views on targeting would evidently have to be given great weight. Although General Hap Arnold and the other American members of the Joint Chiefs of Staff strongly supported Eisenhower in demanding control of the strategic bombers, Spaatz was a man whose views had to be taken into account and which Eisenhower wished to take into account. Moreover, he, like Eisenhower, carried the weapon suggested in the last sentence of the memorandum quoted above—the threat to quit. Spaatz' request for relief from his command would not, of course, have been as explosive as Eisenhower's; but he was the senior U.S. airman in the field, the most experienced, the most respected in both Washington and London. And, in fact, Spaatz once used the threat of resignation (see p. 56, below). Harris, similarly, had to be brought along diplomatically. He had established a quasi-independent status which neither Portal nor Churchill was in a position bluntly to override. On air matters, Portal was close by, representing the Combined Chiefs of Staff, but inclined to back Eisenhower and Tedder even against the views of his own staff.

Churchill, however, was another matter. It was Churchill who held up the formal settlement of the target and command question in the wake of the March 25 meeting. As Eisenhower's memorandum, quoted above, indicated, the command arrangements were contingent on the agreement of an air plan for the support of D-Day, and Churchill did not like Tedder's plan. He appears to have preferred the attack on oil.[23] Unlike Eisenhower, Churchill entered into operational matters in the chains of command below him in the greatest detail.[24] Undoubtedly he was aware of the opposition to Tedder's marshalling-yards plan in the War Office, the Joint Intelligence Committee, MEW, and parts of the Air Ministry, including Bomber Operations. Lord Cherwell, Churchill's scientific adviser, appeared to have preferred bridges to marshalling yards. While suggesting a preference for the attack on oil, Churchill did not propose an alternative transport plan. But he and the British cabinet as a whole challenged the political wisdom of Tedder's plan on the grounds that it would impose extremely heavy civilian casualties on French and Belgian allies, endanger long-run British relations with those countries, and render the subsequent use of the railway net of northwestern Europe difficult for military and civil purposes. In perhaps oblique advocacy of an attack on bridges, the War Cabinet proposed attacks on transport targets only when casualties were not likely to exceed 100–150 persons. Eisenhower stuck to the Tedder plan on grounds of military necessity and the likelihood that Churchill was overestimating civilian casualties on the Continent. Although Eisenhower formally acquired control over the British and American bombers on April 14, the wrangle with Churchill over civilian casualties continued into May when Churchill referred the matter to Roosevelt. The latter backed Eisenhower in a message of May 11.

Thus, Eisenhower and Tedder had their way but, so far as the latter is concerned, only after a fashion.

8. How Oil and Bridges Got In

I kept a cryptic personal diary during my war years in London. The notation for March 26, 1944, when Hughes informed us of the outcome of the high-level meeting of the previous day, reads in part: "A sad and even historic day. We're licked. Marshalling yards. Bet 2 d. they [oil targets] will be attacked—even too late." Oil was flatly turned down as a target system on March 25, and it does not appear in the April 14 directive. Nevertheless, the Fifteenth Air Force began its attacks on the oil refineries at Ploeşti, Romania, on April 5; on May 12 Spaatz attacked a substantial group of oil targets in central Germany, including Leuna. Intelligence, including ULTRA, immediately indicated acute German alarm over these attacks. At the time, Tedder, responding to the intelligence, was reported to have said: "I guess we'll have to give the customer what he wants." And the oil target system was, at last, fully legitimized.[25]

One reason this happened is that the attacks had a much more rapid effect on German military dispositions than any of us had calculated. As indicated above (p. 33), the collective judgment of the oil experts in London was that German stocks amounted to a three-month supply; but, as the quotations cited from the March 25 meeting indicate (pp. 34–35), there was considerable uncertainty about when the attacks would affect German military dispositions. Spaatz' assessment, that the Germans would anticipate shortages and reduce military allocations from the time serious attacks began, proved most nearly correct. As early as May 27 the British Joint Intelligence Sub-committee reported to the War Cabinet that there was evidence of interference, due to oil shortages, of training of combat divisions; a substantial cut in the allocation of oil to the German navy; the outfitting of certain types of motor transport with wood fuel generators; and, most impressive of all at the time, the re-allocation of antiaircraft units protecting three of the principal German aircraft factories, hitherto enjoying highest priority, to protect hydrogenation plants not yet attacked. I suspect this was the item leading to Tedder's remark about giving the customer what he wanted. The fact was that aircraft fuel production, which reached a peak of 180,000 tons in March 1944, was cut to 54,000 tons in June and was down to 10,000 tons in September (see p. 68, below).

This prompt appearance of military consequences in the wake of the few early attacks occurred, in part, because, by the time of the mid-May attack on major synthetic plants, Ploeşti had already been attacked by the Fifteenth Air Force on April 5, 15, and 24. These Romanian attacks came about in a rather curious way, described as follows by Craven and Cate:

> There was, however, a chance to open the oil campaign by dispatching the Fifteenth Air Force to attack the crude-oil refineries around Ploesti, already attacked in the famous mission of August 1943. On 17 March 1944, Arnold notified Spaatz that the Combined Chiefs had no objection to his ordering attacks on Ploesti at the first opportunity, but even so it was thought wise to begin the undertaking surreptitiously under the general directive which called for bombing transportation targets supporting German forces that faced the Russians, who were then breaking into Rumania. Such transportation targets stood in the vicinity of Ploesti, and on 5 April 1944 the Fifteenth Air Force administered an attack on the marshalling yards there with 146 B-24's and 90

B-17's. Most of the 588 tons of bombs, with more than coincidental inaccuracy, struck and badly damaged the Astra group of refineries near by. The Americans did not proclaim the opening of the oil offensive, even in their secret intelligence summaries, but on 15 and 24 April large forces of heavy bombers again attacked Ploesti marshalling yards in the expectation that most of the bombs would produce "incidental" damage to oil refineries. This damage occurred, and to a very encouraging extent.... By 4 May, MAAF headquarters fortified the authority for the Fifteenth Air Force's oil missions by granting permission for them to continue if tactical considerations allowed.[26]

One basis for quiet acquiescence in the attacks on Ploeşti lay in a memorandum of March 31, 1944, from Spaatz to Eisenhower (Appendix C). Accepting the verdict of March 25 with respect to attack on the French railroads, Spaatz argued, in general, that the attack on oil in Germany would prove more beneficial for OVERLORD than attack on the several German marshalling yards included in Tedder's plan: "The effect from the oil attack, while offering a less definite impact in time, is certain to be more far-reaching. It will lead directly to sure disaster for Germany. The rail attack can lead to harassment only." After then pointing out that bombing capabilities existed beyond the needs of currently assigned targets, Spaatz proposed that the transportation lines in the Romanian area be interdicted; if this were done, it would "lend weight to the advantages of early attack upon the Synthetics in order to obtain the earliest possible impact. That impact might well be far earlier than currently estimated."

This odd memorandum can only be understood (*a*) as the effort of a recently defeated group to return to the attack after a week of painful regrouping and (*b*) in the light of knowledge from aerial photographs of the transport facilities serving the Romanian refineries. Tedder's plan restricted the strategic target system assigned to the Fifteenth Air Force to aircraft and transportation. He rightly feared that, if the

Ploeşti refineries were attacked, the case for attacking the oil targets in Germany would be heightened. The marshalling yards at Ploeşti were, however, listed as a legitimate target. What Tedder did not perceive was that each Ploeşti refinery had associated with it a small marshalling yard for parking tanker cars, making up trains, and similar activities. These were, literally, the aiming points chosen in the April 5 attack on Ploeşti. The spacing of the bombs was arranged to enlarge the bombing patterns and overlap onto the nearby refineries.

There was a similar back-door quality to Spaatz' acquiring permission for two pre–D-Day raids on oil plants in central Germany:

> While the Fifteenth Air Force was inaugurating the oil campaign, the way was partly cleared for Eighth Air Force participation....
>
> ... Eisenhower's directive to the strategic air forces on 17 April 1944 gave the German Air Force first priority in USSTAF target listings. The Luftwaffe used oil products and, as AAF Headquarters pointed out, attacks on oil installations could come under the general heading of POINTBLANK without disturbing the Combined Chiefs or the British with efforts to change the existing system of priorities; moreover, the destruction of German fighters which rose to defend the oil plants was undoubtedly a major purpose of the Eighth Air Force. Thus the Eighth Air Force could destroy oil targets, at least as an experiment, while pursuing POINTBLANK, and the Fifteenth Air Force could bomb them under the subterfuge of attacking railway objectives. General Eisenhower, who leaned heavily on Spaatz in air matters, granted verbal permission on 19 April for the bombing of German oil targets on the next two days of good visual conditions. The supreme commander emphasized, as did Spaatz, that the fundamental purpose was to determine the willingness of the Germans to send their fighters against attacking bombers. Somehow it seemed important to the two U.S. leaders not to go on record as taking the initiative in opening this new offensive, which soon would be the pride and chief concern

of the strategic air forces. Tedder, who was in charge of strategic air operations for OVERLORD, momentarily jeopardized the project by insisting upon CROSSBOW [flying bomb launchers] attacks by the Eighth Air Force instead of the oil missions. But a visit of Spaatz to his office on 20 April resulted in a compromise to the effect that one day's effort would be devoted to CROSSBOW, and that the two days of good bombing weather would remain open for the oil plant assaults.[27]

The fact was that Spaatz had proved correct in his predictions that the German fighters would not rise in large numbers to defend the marshalling yards of northwestern Europe and that Eisenhower's caveat on March 25 about the primacy of air supremacy as an objective for D-Day could come into play. It came into play, in part, because Spaatz informed Eisenhower that he would have to relinquish his command if he were not permitted to attack oil targets which, he felt, alone would force the German fighters to engage and thus permit the attrition necessary for Allied air dominance on D-Day.[28] But it was also the case that in a quiet, osmotic way the notion was spreading in the higher echelons of command, in London and Washington, that it had been a mistake on March 25 to postpone the attack on oil.

The attack on the Seine and Meuse bridges before D-Day (and the Loire bridges thereafter) also came about in an unorthodox, faintly comic way.

As late as May 1, 1944, Zuckerman's view, derived from his Mediterranean experience, that the bombing of bridges was excessively costly, still prevailed in AEAF as the following passage of a communication from Leigh-Mallory to Tedder suggests:

> The programme of attacks under this heading, "*Tactical Attacks on Rail Communications*," has not yet been finally agreed. It has been suggested that 5 bridges over the River Seine should be destroyed by bombing, but in view of the heavy expenditure of effort that would be involved (6,000

short tons) and the fact that the lines could be cut at other points (e.g., embankments), for a smaller expenditure of effort, this commitment can be included in the programme of preparatory operations only if the effort can be spared from other essential commitments.[29]

This judgment had long since been overtaken by experience in the Mediterranean:

> With the latter contention [that rail and road bridges were "uneconomical and difficult targets"] the MAAF [Mediterranean Allied Air Forces] Target Section, XII Bomber Command, G-2 of AFHQ, A-2 of Twelfth Air Force, and others were in sharp disagreement.... It seemed apparent that to be effective an interdiction program would have to cut all lines quickly and simultaneously—which could not be accomplished solely by knocking out rail centers. They pointed to a brief period of bridge-busting in late October and early November 1943 which had so successfully cut the main rail lines in central Italy that, according to General D'Aurelio, former chief of the Italian liaison staff with Kesselring, the Germans were "mentally preparing themselves" for a withdrawal to above Rome—and might well have done so had not the Allies abandoned the program before the end of November because of other commitments and bad weather. The exponents of attacks on bridges received a strong boost early in March when an OSS report concluded that an air assault on marshalling yards and repair shops by any force likely to be available in the theater would not produce significant military results, and asserted that "nothing in the record to date shows that a simultaneous interdiction of all north-south rail lines by bombing bridges is beyond the capabilities of MAAF, given a scale of effort comparable to that currently being expended against other transport targets...." On 19 March, MATAF [Mediterranean Allied Tactical Air Forces] issued a definitive directive for the interdiction program, which in code soon was appropriately designated Operation STRANGLE....
>
> The decision to employ large numbers of fighter-bombers

was based upon the principle that the success of STRANGLE would depend upon "simultaneous interdiction," a phrase which meant that, irrespective of whether yards or bridges got top billing, complete interdiction could be achieved only if all lines leading south from the Po Valley were cut simultaneously. . . .

. . . When STRANGLE was no more than two weeks old, Eaker reported that experience had shown the best way to cut lines of communication was by attacks on bridges and viaducts. . . .

As early as 24 March the mediums had cut every through rail line which supplied the German front, and with able assistance from fighter-bombers they kept them cut right through the last day of STRANGLE. . . .

The bridge-busting campaign justified the expectations of its proponents: as early as the middle of April no fewer than 27 bridges had been knocked out; on the vital Rome-Florence line (to use a single example), mediums and fighter-bombers had accomplished full interdiction well before the beginning of the Allied ground offensive in May simply by cutting the main bridges."[30]

As word of these developments was transmitted to London, directly and through visits of high-ranking officers to Italy, advocates of bridge attacks renewed the old debate:

. . . during the spring of 1944 General Spaatz began to urge that experimental attacks be carried out on bridges, for it was apparent that success in this matter would greatly contribute to the transportation campaign. General Brereton likewise pressed for efforts to remove bridges leading toward or into the invasion area. Substantiation for the views of these air generals came out of Italy, where operation STRANGLE showed not only that bridge-breaking was feasible but that it was the most effective way to block the enemy's movements. General Eaker made known the successes of his air forces in sealing off part of the Italian peninsula by means of bridge destruction, and General Anderson brought back from a visit to Italy enthusiastic accounts of the success of

STRANGLE. Pressure for a bridge campaign grew when it was realized that an experimental attack carried out by RAF Typhoons on 21 April 1944 on several French and Belgian bridges had rendered the crossings unusable even if it had failed to destroy them. Soon afterward, on 3 May, Montgomery's headquarters officially requested the air forces to take out several bridges over which the enemy might move reinforcements into Normandy, and his representative subsequently expressed to Leigh-Mallory the view that bridge destruction would be more decisive than "pin-pricking on rail communications." Still there was hesitation. The British railway expert, E. D. Brant, estimated that 1,200 tons would have to be expended on each of the Seine bridges, a costly undertaking which could hardly be afforded in view of other pre-invasion commitments. Leigh-Mallory suggested that Spaatz's heavy bombers attempt the campaign. But Spaatz believed that too much bomb tonnage would be required, since the heavies would have to attack from such high altitudes, and that smaller aircraft, as experience in Italy indicated, were better suited for the task. . . .

On 7 May all serious doubts were swept away by a notable Ninth Air Force operation. Eight P-47's dropped two 1,000-pound bombs apiece on a 650-foot steel railway crossing over the Seine near Vernon and demolished it. This attack, which seems to have been made on Brereton's initiative, was one of four executed that day by P-47's and B-26's. While the Vernon operation was the most clearly successful demonstration, bridges at Oissel, Orival, and Mantes-Gassicourt were badly damaged and soon put out of use. Leigh-Mallory, having thus been convinced that the tactical air forces could do the job, on 10 May directed his forces to begin the destruction of bridges over the Albert Canal and the Meuse River, an enterprise that would suggest Allied concern with the Calais region but would nevertheless help cut off Normandy. SHAEF, alarmed by a report of its G-2 that the rail center bombings were causing only "some slight delay" in enemy rail movements, soon prepared an extensive interdiction program for the air forces which called for cutting all bridges up the Seine to Mantes and up the Loire to Blois and at critical points in the so-called Paris-Orléans gap stretching between the two rivers. . . .

Even so, by 1 June 1944 the enemy's transportation system had still not reached the final state of collapse desired by the Allies, although the 45,000 tons originally allotted for bombing rail centers had been greatly exceeded. The Germans were repairing their bombed marshalling yards and railroad tracks with admirable efficiency, and they were fairly successful in redistributing their traffic flow so as to avoid the worst-damaged points. It seemed that essential military movements were still taking place although much important work, such as the completion of the Atlantic Wall, had to cease because of transportation difficulties. North of the Seine was Field Marshal General Gerd von Rundstedt's large Fifteenth Army, poised to meet an expected assault on Calais. Unless the line of interdiction became perfect, he would probably be able to shift much of his strength into Normandy after D-day. Thus, the best hope of the Allies to seal off the invasion area was to complete the destruction of all twelve railway and fourteen highway bridges over the Seine.

Last-minute attacks on the Seine bridges produced the maximum results: the impassibility of all crossings below Paris. Marauders, Thunderbolts, Lightnings, and Typhoons attacked every day and night, bombing and rebombing until every bridge was unusable. The Germans, of course, made desperate attempts to repair their shattered bridges, but strafing made it difficult and demoralizing work, and even when reconstruction was successful, the Allies would promptly bomb again. Strafing also interfered with the enemy's efforts to unload freight from trains at the broken crossings for ferrying across the Seine to trains on the other side, and the Allies could strand the trains by cutting lines or destroying locomotives. The line of interdiction along the Seine was a fact by D-day.[31]

In the pre–D-Day attacks, tonnage requirements per bridge knocked out proved to be less than one-fifth of Leigh-Mallory's estimate of May 1, that is, 220 versus 1,200.[32]

The bridge target system was, evidently, legitimized by the May 7 experimental attack on the Seine bridge at Vernon. The equivalent of the ULTRA and other intelligence in the wake of the May 12 attack on Leuna and the other synthetic oil plants was a magnificent postattack aerial photograph with the Vernon bridge roadway lying quietly on the bottom of the Seine. On May 8 it was on the desk of every major (and minor) figure concerned with the bombing business. The debate in London on whether bridges could be attacked with reasonable economy was thus settled.

Statistically, however, the result was a sport. The Vernon bridge was dropped in an attack by twelve P-47 (Thunderbolt) fighter bombers, each carrying two 1,000-lb. bombs. (The official attack report is included as Appendix D.) The bridge was, in fact, destroyed by only eight sorties in which the bombs, with delayed fuses, were released at point-blank range, in low-level attacks, into the north and center supports of the bridge. Surplus sorties were directed to a nearby ammunition factory which blew up, throwing debris three thousand feet into the air, severely damaging two of the attacking aircraft. The group chosen for the venture against Vernon and the other bridges targeted for May 7 had been specially trained for this kind of low-level, delayed-fuse attack; but in no sense was this a reasonable statistical test of the likely number of sorties required to damage a bridge severely. And the greatest enthusiasts for bridge busting would not have predicted the result, in which three other bridges were also significantly damaged by the attacking fighter-bomber group.

The official histories are not clear on how the bridge attacks of May 7 actually came about. What we have by way of formal documentary record is thin, indecisive, but not unilluminating. We have the minutes of target planning meetings on May 3 and May 6, 1944, held at Leigh-Mallory's headquarters. At both, bridges as pre–D-Day targets were considered. Here are the four relevant paragraphs summarizing the May 3 discussion:

BRIDGES.

8. As D Day approaches it is recognized that the enemy's lines of communication will become of increasing importance, and if a series of targets could be selected which would cut a number of lines for a period of two to three weeks from D-21 to D Day, this would contribute to the Tactical plan of railway cutting which will be put into force after D Day. It appeared that the Targets which fulfilled this need were Railway Bridges, provided that such attacks were technically practicable, and for this purpose it appeared that the 8th Air Force would be the best force to employ.

9. Professor ZUCKERMAN stated that the result achieved depended on the structure of the bridge, and the type of bomb employed. For this purpose nothing less than the 1,000 lb bomb would be suitable, and preferably the 2,000 lb bomb.

10. It was stated that 21 Army Group were interested in the five SEINE Bridges, but did not want the LOIRE Bridges attacked before D Day, for reasons of security. They would welcome an attack on the SEINE Bridges after about D-15. For security reasons, it was suggested that the MEUSE Bridges might be attacked, in connection with the PAS DE CALAIS area.

11. It was decided that the 8th Air Force should do a full scale attack on three SEINE Bridges and three MEUSE Bridges, any time after D-15. If this was not a success, the final policy would be adjusted. It was felt that the time spent on this attack would not substantially affect the attacks on Railway centres if it did not succeed.

On May 6 Spaatz initiated the discussion by urging that the heavy bombers not be diverted to bridges; but, apparently under pressure from Twenty-first Army Group and the British Second Tactical Air Force, Leigh-Mallory agreed, despite the difficulty of the targets and his fear of wasted effort, that some experimental attacks might be undertaken "between now and D-Day."

BRIDGES.

8. *General Spaatz*, quoting from a Report on Bridge bombing in Italy, said that bridges were repaired very

quickly, unless a span of at least 100′ was demolished. That attacks by heavy bombers were costly, and involved an uneconomic proportion of sorties per bridge damaged. Medium bombers were less costly, and fighter/bombers were most effective. Much depended on the type of construction: masonry was more vulnerable than steel girder construction. The *Air C.-in-C.* said bridges were a difficult target, and he did not want to see a waste of effort at this time. *Brigadier Richardson*, 21 Army Group, said that in addition to the general dislocation achieved by the railway bombing plan, the Army wanted certain specific lines cut on or about D-Day. In particular lines from the AMIENS area and from the LOIRE. He said that the Army wanted 8 bridges destroyed, and felt that this would be of more decisive value than pinpricking on rail communications. *Air Marshal Coningham* said that in the NEPTUNE area M/T was more important to the enemy than railways, and bridges conveyed M/T as well as trains. He was in favour of making experiments in various methods of attacking bridges. The Air *C.-in-C.* agreed that it was worth trying out between now and D-Day what was the most effective method using mediums and fighter/bombers. Bridges on the SEINE and MEUSE (for cover purposes) should be attacked; all were within range of bombers and fighter/bombers of the T.A.F.S. The Eighth would not participate.

Evidently there is something missing here, for there is no suggestion that an experimental attack would be carried out the next day.[33] In my memory and Kindleberger's,[34] the central figure who forced the issue was Brigadier General Frederic H. Smith, Jr., the second-highest ranking U.S. officer (next to General Hoyt S. Vandenberg) assigned to Leigh-Mallory's headquarters. He was present at the meetings of both May 3 and May 6. His memory of the circumstances, as of November 9, 1979, is the following:

> My plan was that we use P-47 fighter-bombers with delayed-action fuses to attack the bridges from the mouth of the Seine to Paris: 1,100-lb. bombs with 3- to 5-second delay fuses. Our thinking was that we could take out all the Seine

63

bridges without tipping off the fact that Normandy was to be our main place of landing. [A systematic attack on the Loire bridges would have indicated, broadly, the landing site.]

Professor Zuckerman, who worked for Sir Trafford Leigh-Mallory, was present. Zuckerman said it would take something like 260 sorties [*sic*] of B-26's per bridge to carry out my plan. I said that's nonsense. [Presumably this occurred at the May 3 meeting.] However, Leigh-Mallory went along with Zuckerman and said no, we will not set those bridges as our objective. In the meantime, word of what I was proposing got to Fred Anderson. The next day he called me and said: "Freddie stay a little later than usual today at your office. A Captain of the Horse Guards will call on you and get your plan for attacking bridges." So when the Captain of the Horse Guards duly arrived, I gave him my plan and went home. Two days later, I believe, Leigh-Mallory said at the morning meeting, Smitty, I have reconsidered your plan and I authorize you to attack a bridge as you desire on the Seine River and we will see what happens. [Presumably this occurred after the May 6 meeting.] So I selected Vernon which was a double-tiered bridge which carried both rail and road traffic. And I called Brigadier General David Schlatter of Ninth Air Force—we lived together—and told him to go ahead. We had discussed this a number of times. Next morning a squadron of P-47's took off from somewhere in the Ninth Air Force with top cover of P-51's, as I remember, and attacked Vernon. The first plane ordered to attack later peeled off and sank his 1,100-lb. bomb in the abutment of the bridge. As he pulled over he saw sympathetic explosions. The Germans had mined it, and the whole thing fell flat in the river. Therefore, I got an okay to go ahead with the Seine bridge target plan as a whole.

I think the Captain of the Horse Guards took the plan to 10 Downing Street and that's where the pressure came from on Leigh-Mallory to reverse his decision. That's my theory.[35]

I shall leave the full story of the shenanigans that introduced the bridges to more compulsive historians who might establish why Fred Anderson of USSTAF and, perhaps, Winston

Churchill or his personal staff got into the act. From our limited point of view in this essay, two facts are significant. First, by early May the weight of Spaatz' command, short of direct and explicit advocacy, was thrown behind the bridge attacks even though it was the tactical rather than strategic aircraft that would be involved. Spaatz' reserved stance of March 25 had ended. The technical success of Operation STRANGLE in Italy was clearly the cause of this shift. Second, as with the oil, Tedder was prepared to shift his position as the evidence came in. His commentary on the bridges in his memoir is terse but candid: "The rail and road bridges began to receive attention. Though expert opinion, with which I had concurred, had earlier held these targets to be relatively unprofitable for attack, our bomber crews now surpassed even their own standards."[36]

And so, by D-Day bridges and oil as well as railroad centers were legitimate target systems. In an odd, up-hill battle the apparent decision of March 25 had been radically altered; and the mixture of target systems which evolved between March 25 and D-Day persisted over the next three months, with a distinguished contribution to the oil offensive from RAF Bomber Command.

9. The Neoclassical Period: September 1944-May 1945

The battle over policy did not, however, end. Although our concern here is rather narrowly with Eisenhower's March 25 decision, the subsequent course of events, well detailed in the official histories, is broadly relevant to an evaluation of that decision.

On September 1, 1944, the Combined Chiefs of Staff returned the heavy bombers to control of their own staffs, that is, to USSTAF and Air Ministry, Whitehall. This formally, at least, ended the period of direct control by SHAEF and AEAF, the latter being disbanded in October and its personnel becoming SHAEF (Air). A central advisory co-ordinating committee was set up: the Combined Strategic Target Committee (CSTC). EOU was formally represented on the CSTC. Staff arguments previously conducted through higher-level intermediaries now took place directly across the table. In fact, of course, SHAEF—in effect Tedder—was still in a powerful position to affect the pattern of heavy-bomber operations.

The period between September 1944 and V-E Day falls into three phases. In the first period, of about two months, when the Allied armies were advancing rapidly through France, the transport targets previously assigned were literally overrun; with this drain lifted, the heavy bombers, including RAF Bomber Command, devoted themselves to oil as a clear-cut first priority. In addition, a Military Supplies Working Committee was set up, with Lawrence as chairman and Kaysen as secretary, to array tank, truck, and depot targets. For a time it appeared as if the war might end with a straightforward program of military attack on oil and weapons. But the advocates of marshalling-yard attacks at SHAEF (Air) and SHAEF G-2 counterattacked successfully toward the end of October, and the attack on military supplies was sacrificed. The last meeting of the Military Supplies Working Committee was held on October 23. Transport attacks in Germany were now justified on the strategic grounds that they reduced German military production as well as in terms of their believed effects on the movement to the battlefronts of German military forces and supplies.

In the second period, running roughly from the end of October to Field Marshal Karl von Rundstedt's counteroffensive of December, bombing policy was affected by the belief that the end of the war was imminent. SHAEF (Air) sponsored, throughout that period, and the Air Staffs acquiesced in what was believed to be a short-run heavy-bomber policy, namely, attack on German marshalling yards, both proximate and distant from the battle area. The exact mechanism by which such attacks were expected to hasten decision on the ground was not clear; but the sponsors of the attacks undoubtedly hoped for general economic and military confusion on a scale such as to cause capitulation. From this view EOU dissented. Throughout this period oil, nominally still in top priority for the heavy bombers, was somewhat neglected; and the Germans achieved some revival of production as a result of a truly extraordinary repair effort, as Table 2 indicates. Very massive tonnage figures were piled up against the German rail system, and, as noted above, the attack on military supplies was virtually abandoned.

As Appendix E indicates, a rethinking of bombing policy began during the slowdown of the Allied advance in the late autumn. But the Rundstedt counteroffensive forced revision. It had two sobering effects. First, it showed that a concentrated transport attack, in a limited area proximate to the front,

Table 2. Monthly German Production and Imports of Total Finished Oil Products and Aircraft Fuel, January 1944–March 1945[a] (*In thousand metric tons*)

Year and Month	Synthetic Production		Domestic Refining of Crude Oil	Production in Occupied Territories	Imports	Total	Aircraft Fuel
	Hydrogenation and Fischer-Tropsch Process	Other Synthetic Production					
1944							
January	336	162	175	48	179	900	160
February	306	172	160	48	200	886	164
March	341	201	191	49	186	968	180
April	348	153	157	48	104	810	175
May	285	151	170	47	81	734	156
June	145	153	129	44	40	511	54
July	86	143	115	38	56	438	35
August	47	137	134	16	11[b]	345	17
September	26	126	113	5	11	281	10
October	38	117	124	3	34	316	21
November	78	107	105	10	37	337	39
December	56	108	108	9	22	303	25
1945							
January	37	*	*	*	*	*	*
February	13	*	*	*	*	*	*
March	12	*	*	*	*	*	*

Source: This table is drawn from tables in Webster and Frankland, *Strategic Air Offensive against Germany,* IV, 516–517.

[a] U.S. Strategic Bombing Survey, "The Effects of Strategic Bombing on the German War Economy," table 41, p. 79; sources: *Produktion der Hydrier und Synthese Werke* in 1000 moto, chart prepared by Dr. Butefisch, May 1945, and *Statistische Schnellberichte zur Kriegsproduktion,* Planungsamt, Ministry for Armament and War Production.

[b] The Russians occupied Ploești on August 22, 1944.

could achieve significant military results. The whole of the bomber forces had been thrown into a limited number of carefully selected points, at the base of the German salient, when the weather cleared just before Christmas 1944.[37] These bomber attacks, strongly supported by the fighter-bombers, were effective in denying the flow of supplies forward to the German spearheads; and the lesson was read that transport attacks should be limited to systematic efforts to wreck or interdict the transport system in the area immediately behind the front. The bogey (as seen by EOU) of strategic general attack on rail transport was almost, but not quite, laid.

Second, the counteroffensive, in suggesting strongly that the war was not yet over, led to the re-introduction of tanks, jet aircraft, ordnance depots, and other target systems of a military character; and, above all, it brought oil back into fairly effective first priority. The Military Supplies Working Committee was reinstated early in 1945 with Barnett of EOU as chairman.

The debate nevertheless continued between the advocates of attritional versus interdiction attacks on transport. SHAEF persisted in advocacy of strategic attack on transport, while the Air Ministry, War Office, EOU, and MEW fought for a limited tactical program of attack. The effectiveness of the Ardennes transport bombing strengthened the hand of the latter group and resulted finally in the Ruhr interdiction scheme, which emerged from protracted and harrowing negotiation between the divergent schools.

In this third phase a further issue was posed by the Russian advance to the Oder, and the crossing of the Rhine by the American First and Third Armies. With these movements came the evident approach of an end to formal hostilities. At peak strength, capable of bombing anywhere in German Europe without serious opposition, heavy bomber forces sought new means to bring the war to a close. The oil program contained relatively few targets, and these were battered and unattractive. The Ruhr interdiction scheme was virtually complete and soon outmoded by the crossing of the Rhine by the Twenty-first Army Group. Area raids on Berlin, Dresden, and Chemnitz were carried out by the Eighth Air Force in conjunction with RAF Bomber Command; a large number of small central German marshalling yards were hit in two spectacular medium-level operations (called CLARION); but no key could be found to a truly decisive use of air power at this stage.

It was the EOU view that no key existed: that, since heavy bombers could not be used, with existing techniques, in close army support, they should continue to do thoroughly the oil and military supply targets, capable of affecting the battle over short periods, and, if possible, serve as transport aircraft to fast-moving ground columns. EOU opposed the bombing of Dresden and Chemnitz.

The last serious planning battle of the war took place between the old antagonists, fighting with old weapons, on familiar grounds. In April 1945 SHAEF (Air) advocated the attack on a large number of marshalling yards throughout the length of the central area of Germany still held by German forces. The aim of these attacks was "to exert pressure on the enemy." It was agreed that they could not stop military movements south to the Redoubt Area (Bavarian Alps) or have any other clear-cut military effect. EOU and the majority of the CSTC advocated attack on the last of the oil plants and on the ordnance depots, on which the retreating Germans were falling back and drawing for supplies. They felt it was intrinsic to the nature of strategic bombing that, so far as the heavy bombers were concerned, in the second war against Germany, air operations should end not with a bang but a whimper.

The issue was settled, with some acrimony and strain on civility among the staffs represented on the CSTC, by a decision of the air commanders that the SHAEF transport plan would be carried out. EOU and the dissident members of CSTC retired, of course, from the fray, gaining some wry comfort, however, from the fact that a sudden advance of the armies eliminated the bulk of the proposed targets before attack could be mounted.

10. A Few Conclusions

Two characteristics of Eisenhower's decision of March 25, 1944, would appear to be that it was made between false alternatives and that the decision did not stick. A decision was made to attack marshalling yards and to postpone the question of attack on oil until after D-Day. There was no place in the decision for a systematic attack on bridges. But within two weeks the attack on oil had begun; and a month before D-Day the systematic attack on bridges was launched.

One result of this outcome is that it is extremely difficult to sort out with confidence the relative effects of each form of attack on the German military performance on D-Day and in the critical weeks beyond. (Appendix F provides a contemporary evaluation as of D plus 13.) After all, bridges, marshalling yards, and oil are all instruments of transport. And if one takes the rate of the defensive German buildup in Normandy as a criterion for the effectiveness of these converging efforts, one must also allow for the deception plan which pinned many German divisions in the Pas de Calais, the operations of the French underground, and the fighters which, starting on May 2, shot up locomotives and other transport targets with enthusiasm. It is not surprising, then, that the official military historians find difficult a firm evaluation of the relative efficacy of the various forms of air attack launched before D-Day.[38]

William F. Whitmore, an operations analyst rather than a

historian, has made perhaps the most serious effort to sort out what happened. His "Logistics as a Target System" is about as precise and objective an effort to arrive at a definitive conclusion as is likely to be made.[39] He was one of eight civilians who made an early analysis on behalf of the AAF Evaluation Board, ETO, of the relative efficacy of attritional versus interdiction transport attacks before D-Day as part of the preparation for the U.S. invasion of Japan then envisaged. His summary of the basic conclusions of the Evaluation Board report follows:

> An attrition attack on rail centers is estimated to have cut rail traffic 30 percent by 20 May 1944 and another 27 percent by the middle of July. Rail cuts alone may have accounted for some 19 percent in the same interval, but with some overlap, since some rail cuts were made in centers. Thus, the attrition attack is credited with 70 percent of the observed 77 percent decline, the remainder being credited to sabotage action. Other results were:
> 1. A 33 percent cut in utilizable locomotives. But enough remained to handle the traffic desired—some were even requisitioned for German lines.
> 2. A 14-day coal reserve dropped to one day by the time of the St. Lo breakthrough.
> 3. Rolling stock dropped 20 percent; again satisfactory, except for spot shortages of special cars, which forced a Panzer Division to drive its tanks 400 miles under their own power; turn-around time in yards was doubled.
> 4. Injury to repair and servicing facilities never became critical, but there was general disorganization of a rather rigid administrative system.
>
> All this seriously hampered the flow of traffic, but it did not stop essential military supplies. Troop trains ran at an undiminished rate.
>
> In contrast to this picture, an interdiction campaign was scheduled by SHAEF G-2, based on three sets of bridges plus track cuts (though these were not systematically integrated into the interdiction lines). The first line included the Seine-

Loire bridges west of Paris, isolating the Normandy invasion area. The second ran east of Paris, cutting off routes from Belgium and Germany. The third was farther east, toward Belgium, and was never effectively attacked. The first line was effectively established, receiving over ten times the bomb tonnage of the second line; the second was not. The routes crossing the first line were cut for 79 percent of the 70-day period following D-Day; for the second line, the figure was only 27 percent. It was estimated that German tactical needs would have been met by 24 trains per day across the first line and 30 trains per day across the second. They got less than one train a day over the first line (actually, none at all during the period D-plus-5 to D-plus-35). Even if the trains had crossed the line, only eight per day could be moved within the area because of the track-cutting campaign. About 52 trains of all types per day moved over the second line, of which 27 were devoted to German tactical traffic out of 30 desired. The discrepancy of three trains a day was caused by sudden concentrated requirements.

Thus, the Germans were vulnerable to attacks on their rail transportation. This was reduced by attrition attacks, but not to a crippling level. Interdiction attacks isolated the invasion area for two months, preventing German reinforcements from destroying the beachhead and contributing to the breakthrough toward Paris.[40]

But the debate, for those still interested, will continue. As Kindleberger said in his review of Zuckerman's memoir: "A more serious irony of history is that Nature does not conduct controlled experiments. Frequently when protagonists have long debated alternative courses of action, decision is taken to do both, so that it is impossible to tell in retrospect which course was right."[41] One is tempted, especially since things turned out reasonably well, to conclude that there was some higher wisdom in letting, in the end, all the protagonists do what they, for whatever reasons, so passionately wanted to do.

But there are a few fairly unchallengeable conclusions to be drawn from this tale which make it a bit difficult to end on so benign a note.

First, the intellectual side of the debate. The effort to justify the attack on the marshalling yards of northwestern Europe on the basis of the 1943 experience in Sicily and southern Italy does not hold water: the circumstances and timing of events and requirements in the two theaters were different; the size and resilience of the railroad systems to be attacked were not comparable; and, as anyone willing to read the text of the evaluation of the 1943 attacks can confirm, the factual analysis in no way justified the broad and firm propositions to be found in the report's summary and conclusions. For example, the text of the report (pp. 56–57) states that in September–October 1943, 4,500 tons of bombs were employed in attacks on rail and road bridges, cutting or "half-destroying" twelve, blocking or otherwise impeding traffic in fifteen other cases. A crude but conservative estimate would have suggested something like 375 tons were required per bridge, rather than the 1,200 tons which became the conventional wisdom. The same broad conclusion emerges from the application of regression analysis to the data in the Sicily report.[42]

Thus a clear-cut error was, without quesion, made. Even before Tedder and Zuckerman departed the Mediterranean for London, the possibility of efficient bridge attacks had been demonstrated, as they were to be demonstrated on a large scale in Operation STRANGLE in February and March 1944. It should not have required the protracted conspiratorial endeavor leading up to the serendipitous attack on Vernon on May 7 to alter policy.

So far as support for the invasion was concerned, the bridge advocates got a good deal of what they wanted, although, as Whitmore notes, the third, easternmost ring of bridges was never effectively attacked and the second not as thoroughly as the first. The interdictionists can continue to argue, as some have argued, that the marshalling-yard attacks were unnecessary; that the rate of buildup of German forces would have been no different if only bridges and a few critical junctions had been attacked; and that it might have been slower if time had been allowed for all three rings of bridges to be attacked. But even the most passionate opponent of the marshalling yards can argue that the technical effects of those attacks at the time had negative military consequences.[43] The major cost of Tedder's transport plan was that, in all its consequences, it postponed the attack on oil: it not only diverted the heavy bombers to other targets, but the controversy was so intense that it also generated pressures to prevent oil attacks with strategic forces not required for marshalling-yard attacks. And, in general, it is with respect to the postponement of oil that the consequences of the March 25 decision appear most serious.

To this outcome a second quite substantial intellectual error contributed. The error was made by the Anglo-American oil experts, including EOU taken as a collectivity, that is, including myself. In calculating the timing of the effect of the attack on oil on German military dispositions, they stuck, rather mechanically, to their measurement of the size of stocks relative to the estimated rate of German military consumption.[44] In fact, the Germans, quite capable of doing arithmetic, began almost immediately to anticipate the consequences on future availabilities of current losses in oil production yielding a much quicker military effect than was initially estimated. In addition, the calculations were not sufficiently disaggregated. As Table 2 shows, aircraft fuel was brought down to disastrous levels by June. If this dynamic process had been clearly perceived and persuasively presented, in disaggregated terms, Eisenhower and Portal would not have been confronted with the disparate statements on timing of Spaatz, Anderson, and Lawrence on March 25, the latter virtually deciding the matter in Tedder's favor as Portal immediately perceived. Undoubtedly those who advocated the attack on oil wished to be professional and cautious in their assessment of the timing of its consequences for German military effectiveness on D-Day and immediately thereafter; but in failing to dramatize effectively the promptness with which a current and prospective decline in oil production would alter German military plans and dispositions, they reinforced a political situation among the top military commanders which was, in itself, exceedingly costly. Here the ultimate problem lay, for, after all, staff advisers do not make command decisions.

One cannot reconstruct the problem of Eisenhower dealing with Tedder, Spaatz, Leigh-Mallory, and Churchill, or Portal dealing with Tedder, Spaatz, and Harris, without feeling for them a certain compassion. Effective power was so diffused among these quasi-autonomous figures in the extraordinary circumstances of Europe in 1944 that Eisenhower, and Portal as well, was forced to operate on what might be called the Charlie Curtis principle: "It may be that truth is best sought in the market of free speech, but the best decisions are neither bought nor sold. They are the result of disagreement, where the last word is not 'I admit you're right,' but 'I've got to live with the son of a bitch, haven't I.'"[45] This healing precept may be fundamental to the successful workings of political democracy in times short of crisis; but it is not necessarily the optimum process for making military decisions.

A highly centralized, effective command structure and process might, of course, have yielded a worse result: bridges might have been totally excluded and oil postponed still further. As Andrew Goodpaster observed in a letter to me of April 8, 1980, responding to a draft of this book: ". . . the somewhat messy process by which the attack on bridges and on oil finally came into being is testimony to the value of a degree of flexibility, pragmatism and open-mindedness—rather than rigidity or preconceptions based on deficient analysis. I would suggest that the art of command is knowing where flexibility descends into mere muddling and indecision. Since the events finally turned out 'right,' although late and at greater cost, I would assume it was 'flexibility' that we were seeing, along with some understandable limitations reflecting less than perfect knowledge." Nevertheless, as things turned out, with the benefit of hindsight and the most careful mobilization of evidence by disinterested parties, the delay in the attack on oil must be accounted a costly result of Eisenhower's March 25 decision, flexible and responsive as it proved to be.

Albert Speer's memoir opens its twenty-fourth chapter with this rather Wagnerian passage: "On May 8, 1944, I returned to Berlin to resume my work. I shall never forget the date May 12, four days later. On that day the technological war was decided. Until then we had managed to produce approximately as many weapons as the armed forces needed, in spite of their considerable losses. But with the attack of nine hundred and thirty-five daylight bombers of the American Eighth Air Force upon several fuel plants in central and eastern Germany, a new era in the air war began. It meant the end of German armaments production."[46] Speer's earlier testimony, comparing the relative strategic results of oil and transportation attacks, is more precise: "As a result of the losses in the fuel industry it was no longer possible even in December 1944 and January 1945 to make use of the reduced armaments production in the battle. The loss of fuel had, in my opinion, therefore, a more decisive effect on the course of the war than the difficulties in armaments and communications."[47]

Galland elaborates Speer's view as follows:

> The most successful operation of the entire Allied strategical air warfare was against the German fuel supply. This was actually the fatal blow for the Luftwaffe! Looking back, it is difficult to understand why the Allies started this undertaking so late, after they had suffered such heavy losses in other operations. . . .

> As early as June, 1944, the month the invasion started, we felt very badly the effects of the consolidated offensive. Fuel production suddenly sank so low that it could no longer satisfy the urgent demands. Speer, when interrogated by the Allies, stated that from June on, it had been impossible to get enough aviation fuel. While it was possible with the greatest effort to keep up at least a minimum production of motor and diesel fuel, the repair work on the plants where normal fuel was converted to octane constituted difficulties which were impossible to overcome. The enemy soon found out how much time we needed for reconstruction and for resuming production. Shortly before this date was reached under tremendous strain came the next devastating raid.
>
> By applying the strictest economy measures and by using the reserves of the OKW (Western High Command), it was possible to continue the fuel supply to the army during the summer months of 1944. Yet from September on, the shortage of petrol was unbearable. The Luftwaffe was the first to be hit by this shortage. Instead of the minimum of 160,000 tons monthly, only 30,000 tons of octane could be allotted. Air force operations were thereby made virtually impossible! For the army similarly disastrous conditions did not arise before the winter.
>
> The raids of the Allied air fleets on the German petrol supply installations was the most important of the combined factors which brought about the collapse of Germany.[48]

Postwar analysts and historians are, indeed, virtually unanimous in their verdict that the attack on oil represented the most effective use of strategic air power in the European theater, although it absorbed less than 10 percent of the tonnage dropped by USSTAF in the period January 1944– May 1945, as opposed to 43 percent allocated to land transport. It is hard to avoid the conclusion that the oil offensive should have been begun at the earliest possible time, in the wake of the Big Week of late February; it is clear that it could have been pursued without significant loss to the pre–D-Day transport attacks, including the bridges and rail lines; and it should have been pursued relentlessly by the RAF Bomber Command as well as the Eighth and Fifteenth Air Forces. In his own way, Harris, long a redoubtable opponent of oil, is generous in retrospect as well as justly proud of the contribution ultimately made to the oil offensive by his command:

> In the spring of 1944 the Americans began a series of attacks against German synthetic oil plants, and a week after D-Day Bomber Command was directed to take part in the same campaign by attacking the ten synthetic oil plants situated in the Ruhr. At the time, I was altogether opposed to this further diversion, which, as I saw it, would only prolong the respite which the German industrial cities had gained from the use of the bombers in a tactical role; I did not think that we had any right to give up a method of attack which was indisputably doing the enemy enormous harm for the sake of prosecuting a new scheme the success of which was far from assured. In the event, of course, the offensive against oil was a complete success, and it could not have been so without the co-operation of Bomber Command, but I still do not think that it was reasonable, at that time, to expect that the campaign would succeed; what the Allied strategists did was to bet on an outsider, and it happened to win the race.[49]

But, in fact, Harris gave Portal a hard time over oil. Despite his retrospective acquiescence, it proved impossible at the time to harness the combined bomber forces in a sustained way to the oil offensive. The nominal priority for oil which emerged after D-Day was systematically eroded by Tedder's hankering for transportation, Harris' for city-busting. Total concentration on oil targets would have been impossible to sustain for reasons of weather and irreducible tactical diversions in support of the ground battle. But there were, in effect, two setbacks to the oil offensive: one, the delay between, say, early March and mid-May, as the debate preceding the March 25 decision ate up the clock and the negative March 25 decision on oil was laboriously undone; the other, the dilution of oil priority, notably in the autumn of 1944 with consequences to be observed in Table 2. After examining in great detail how this diffusion of effort arose, Webster and Frankland pose the ultimate question:

> Could this result [the virtual elimination of oil production] have been obtained two or three months earlier if a greater effort had been made in the autumn to complete the destruction of the remaining Bergius hydrogenation and Fischer-Tropsch plants? There can be no certain answer to this question because no one can say exactly how successful the attempt would have been or how far it would have reduced the German resistance. But as has been seen . . . there seems to have been at least a fair chance that the attacks would have been almost as successful in October and November as they undoubtedly were in December and January.
>
> In December also the attention of the strategic forces was diverted to the protection of the armies during the Ardennes offensive. Had that offensive not taken place undoubtedly more attacks would have been made on the oil targets. How many could have been made in the three months October–December if Sir Arthur Harris had had the same view of the situation as Sir Charles Portal it is impossible to say. In any case some production would have been possible in the smaller plants and the distilleries. But if the supply of aviation spirit could have been prevented from rising above the September level, the *Luftwaffe* might have been in almost the same position by the end of January as it in fact was three months later.
>
> It is by no means certain that this would have stopped altogether the Ardennes offensive for the final stocks might have been used for that purpose. Nor would it have induced the Russians to resume their offensive on the main Eastern front for their inaction was due to other causes. In any case the Germans would have prolonged this resistance by the stubborn fighting of their infantry as they did in the final stages of the war. All that can be said is that, if it had been possible to press home the attack earlier, there can be little

doubt that the collapse of Germany would have come sooner.

It is thus hardly possible not to agree with the judgment which Sir Charles Portal had at the time that neglect of the opportunities provided by the oil offensive might prolong the war for several months. . . . this view was shared neither by Sir Arthur Harris nor by some others in a position to influence the objectives of the attack. Fortunately when Sir Charles Portal made the observation the turning point had already come. But had it come earlier the unreasoning pessimism of the Western Alliance in January might have been avoided and the more optimistic view of October might have continued to persist. In this case less thought would have been given to using the strategic air forces to assist the Russian offensive and more to winning a rapid victory in the West. If this could have been achieved not only would many German and Allied lives been saved, but there would also have been political consequences of great importance to the future of Europe. So great were the stakes of the oil offensive.[50]

If one adds to Webster and Frankland's "several months" lost in the autumn of 1944 the several months lost between, say, March 1 and mid-May, the cost of delay and diversion may have been high. In terms of Table 2, the counterfactual question is: How would the war have gone if German oil availabilities at the September 1944 low point had been achieved by June, say, 200,000 tons over-all, 10,000 tons of aircraft fuel? The costs of failing to produce this result may have been high not only in human life foregone but also in terms of postwar diplomacy; for, in the end, the location of the Soviet and Western armies on V-E Day certainly played a role—the extent of which can be debated—in leading Stalin to conceive as realistic the creation of a Soviet empire in Eastern Europe, yielding a split, intensively armed continent, rather than a united but disarmed Germany, with democracy free to flourish in the East as well as the West. That, presumably, is the grand issue raised in the last two sentences of Webster and Frankland's summation—an issue whose complexities are explored in the second and third essays of this series.

Ultimately, then, Eisenhower's decision of March 25 must be viewed along with two other decisions which may have contributed to the failure to end the war in 1944: his decision not to force Field Marshal Bernard Montgomery to clear the port of Antwerp at whatever cost, immediately upon the city's capture on September 4, 1944; and his decision not to throw his limited paratroop units, oil supplies, and transport facilities behind either Montgomery or General George Patton in the autumn campaign. It must be acknowledged, however, that Montgomery's style did not lend itself well to such an all-out thrust; and to have backed Patton at the expense of Montgomery would have created painful strains with the British. All three of Eisenhower's decisions are thus wholly understandable for a commander instructed to defeat the Germans while holding together a political coalition—not merely an Anglo-American coalition, but a coalition of bomber barons and idiosyncratic ground-force commanders in the field. Eisenhower's capacity to live with the "sons of bitches" and get them to live with each other was, after all, one reason for his choice as commanding general. And while Churchill perceived that where the armies stood on V-E Day might have considerable significance for the Western bargaining position vis-à-vis Moscow, Roosevelt either did not or decided to put his faith in a less contentious postwar relationship with the USSR to be worked out starting from the distribution of the German occupation zones negotiated within the European Advisory Commission.

As for the March 25 decision, Eisenhower's memorandum for the record (see pp. 48–49 above) suggests strongly that what he was seeking that day was "a satisfactory answer" which would resolve the command conflicts which had bedeviled him for several months rather than an optimum use of air power. He did not question sharply the participants at that meeting on the assumptions underlying their judgments and the grounds for those assumptions. In retrospect, there is a haunting quality to Spaatz' clear perception, at the March 25 meeting and in his March 31 memorandum to Eisenhower, that the oil attack would achieve quicker military results than the oil experts' measurement of stocks suggested. Nor did Eisenhower do the thing which marks great executives: probe hard to widen the range of options that Tedder, Spaatz, and Harris—each for his own reasons—laid before him on that day. He decided among those options, letting oil and bridges slide in and Harris' bombers come to play a precision bombing role in the transport and oil attacks out of the dynamics of events he did not control, but in which he acquiesced.

One's judgment of Eisenhower in this matter—and the other two decisions cited which may have delayed victory in Europe—depends on one's criteria. The Smuts criterion would exonerate him. In his memoir John Slessor reports the following: "General Smuts once said to me, 'My boy, it is the greatest mistake to imagine that it is the great victories that decide wars; on the contrary, it is the great blunders. We ought, for instance, to erect a statue to Hitler in Trafalgar Square for having been such a fool as to attack Russia.'"[51] In terms of the war against Germany, Eisenhower did not make any "great blunders." He fulfilled the directive given him and received the German surrender. On the other hand, it seems clear that he did not enter deeply into the problem of how the massive air power entrusted to him should be disposed, did not form a clear judgment of his own and impose it. A non-Smuts view of a commanding general's responsibilities would regard his performance in this respect as inadequate; for, lacking firm control, the use of Allied air power in 1944–1945 was substantially less effective than it might have been. And this was not accidental. Eisenhower had a clear notion of how leadership should be exercised in a complex bureaucracy that he once set down in these terms:

> The military methods and machinery for making and waging war have become so extraordinarily complex and intricate that high commanders must have gargantuan staffs for control and direction.... But personal characteristics are more important than ever before in warfare. The reasons for this are simple. It was not a matter of great moment if a Wellington happened to be a crusty, unapproachable individual who found one of his chief delights in penning sarcastic quips to the War Office. He was the single head, who saw the whole battlefield and directed operations through a small administrative staff and a few aides and orderlies. As long as he had the stamina and the courage to make decisions and to stand by them, and as long his tactical skill met the requirements of his particular time and conditions, he was a great commander. But the teams and staffs through which the modern commander absorbs information and exercises his authority must be a beautifully interlocked, smooth-working mechanism. Ideally, the whole should be practically a single mind; consequently misfits defeat the purpose of the command organization essential to supply and control of the vast land, air, sea, and logistical forces that must be brought to bear as a unity against the enemy.[52]

In fact, the Allied air forces did not quite operate as "a beautifully interlocked, smooth-working mechanism"; but then no human institution, in fact, does. Eisenhower operated more nearly on the Curtis principle, which is what romantic conceptions of bureaucratic order generally come to. In the context of the Second World War in Europe during 1944, that principle had its costs as well as merits.

Now a final observation which should have imposed—and should impose—an important degree of modesty on those who argued and may argue in the future about the use of air power in Europe during the Second World War. Air power helped mightily to win the war. Indeed, the war was almost certainly not winnable without mastery over the German fighter force and virtually total air supremacy over the battlefield on D-Day and in the critical period of consolidating the Normandy bridgehead on the Continent. The pre–D-Day attacks on the bridges and dumps and the direct attack on enemy forces after D-Day certainly helped ease—and ease substantially—the task of the men fighting on the ground. The attacks on oil and military production targets in Germany certainly helped. The attacks on transport centers in Germany, although less productive, in my view, than a more persistent and concentrated attack on oil, certainly had an impact on military as well as civil production and other diffuse but not trivial military effects. Something of the same could be said for the area bombing of German cities. But the ultimate fact is that the war had to be won on the ground by the armies.

F. M. Sallagar makes the point temperately and well in a 1972 study of Operation STRANGLE.[53] In specifying the precise effects of the technically successful interdiction of railway lines in Italy, Sallagar notes that in one way or another essential military supplies did get through even if mainly by road. What the air attacks did was radically to reduce the mobility of the German forces and significantly impair their effectiveness in many other rather impressive ways;[54] but they did not achieve the airman's dream of rendering unnecessary the bloody struggle on the ground.

This certainly proved to be the case with respect to OVERLORD and its aftermath. The buildup of the German forces against the beachhead was slower than it would have been without prior bombing attacks and consistent harassment; German units often arrived piecemeal at the front after incredible difficulties and significant depletion; but they arrived and fought, postponing for eight weeks the breakout from the Normandy peninsula, and after the disheveled retreat across France in mid-summer and early autumn, they fought hard again, postponing final defeat until eleven months after D-Day. There is something pathetic as well as understandable in the various schemes and enterprises to use air power "decisively" in the final weeks of the war. Despite as massive nonnuclear air power as is ever likely to be assembled, the bombers remained to the end a supporting force to the infantry, although all three doctrines had their chance: marshalling yards, area bombing, and oil. In retrospect, I am glad EOU understood and accepted with some perspective and maturity—but without loss of ardor —the limits as well as the possibilities of the enterprise in which its members were privileged to play a part.

So far as the narrow theme of this book is concerned, the saga is a remarkable demonstration of the power of abstract intellectual concepts over the emotions of men and the behavior of institutions. It is not a unique phenomenon, but it is not often that deeply felt debate over rival concepts persists among men in their seventh and eighth decades thirty-five years after the days when their clash had operational meaning and consequence.

Appendix A.
Final Minutes of the March 25 Meeting

[*Note*: Spaatz felt the initial draft of the minutes seriously misrepresented his views. McMullen, Kennedy, and Lawrence also asked for changes. This is the final, amended version.]

C.A.S./Misc./61 (Final).

FINAL MINUTES OF A MEETING HELD ON SATURDAY MARCH 25TH TO DISCUSS THE BOMBING POLICY IN THE PERIOD BEFORE "OVERLORD"

The following were present:—

Marshal of the R.A.F. Sir Charles Portal	—C.A.S.
General Eisenhower	—S.A.C.A.E.F.
Air Chief Marshal Tedder	—Deputy S.A.C.A.E.F.
Air Chief Marshal Leigh-Mallory	—Air C.-in-C. A.E.A.F.
Air Chief Marshal Harris	—A.O.C.-in-C. Bomber Command
Lt. General Spaatz Major General Anderson	—U.S.ST.A.F.
Major General Kennedy Major General McMullen Major General Crawford	—War Office
Air Marshal Bottomley Air Vice-Marshal Inglis	—Air Ministry

Sir Andrew Noble	—J.I.S.
Mr. Lawrence	—M.E.W.
Mr. Crawford	—P.S. to C.A.S. (Secretary)

C.A.S. explained the circumstances in which the meeting had been called and then asked A.C.M. Tedder to explain the nature of his bombing plan.

A.C.M. Tedder said that his plan was based on two principles:

(a) That G.A.F. [German air force] targets should remain on the highest priority and that everything necessary should be done to keep G.A.F. production and strength on as low a figure as possible.

There was agreement by all present that this priority should be maintained and that the purpose of the meeting was to consider what target system ought to be attacked with the effort remaining after what was necessary had been allotted to the attack of G.A.F. targets. It was confirmed that G.A.F. targets included enemy ball-bearing factories.

(b) That the remaining effort should be used to delay and disorganise enemy ground movements both during and after the "NEPTUNE" [the amphibious operations within OVERLORD] assault so as to help the Army to get ashore and stay ashore. He proposed that the target system of second priority should be the enemy's railway system. According to his plan the target of first priority within this railway system should be the enemy's railway servicing centres; he was convinced that a concerted attack on these would reduce the efficiency of the enemy railway system which was already severely strained to a very low level. By doing this it was hoped that we should force the enemy to pass all traffic in the OVERLORD area through a comparatively small number of lines and the task of the tactical air forces of cutting these critical lines after D day would be very much simplified; we should also be able to reduce very considerably the efficiency and flexibility of his repair services and so make it much harder for him to repair quickly the damage inflicted in the tactical battle. The result would be that in the first few weeks of OVERLORD the enemy's railway movement would suffer considerable delays and he would be forced to move formations by road which would be very much slower than by rail.

A.C.M. Tedder said that he did not wish to claim too much for the plan. In particular, he did not claim that the attacks on the servicing centres and marshalling yards would prevent all traffic getting through. He was however convinced that without the all-out attack that he proposed the tactical plan for the disorganization of enemy movement immediately before and after D day would have no chance of success.

C.A.S. said that he felt sure that all were agreed that the execution of this plan would have a most serious effect on the efficiency of the enemy railway system. It was essential however to be certain that what was left would not be adequate for the amount of movement which the enemy would find necessary in the first few weeks of the battle, bearing in mind that he must possess large stocks in N. France and that much of the present traffic was civil and not military and would undoubtedly be severely curtailed once the battle started.

Considerable discussion ensued on this question.

General McMullen said that the railways in North France were in some ways very vulnerable depending as they did to a considerable extent on a steady flow of coal obtained in the Lille/Lens area which had to be collected in wagons in railway storage yards and then distributed. These storage yards presented good targets. At the same time it must be remembered that the Germans were already using 45,000 military railwaymen on the French railways and that even though we destroyed the permanent servicing facilities they could quickly put up in a few days a number of small temporary servicing units with the essential facilities required to keep railway equipment going. He was doubtful as to how much the plan of strategical bombing could reduce the overall efficiency of the system, but even if this produced a reduction to between 20 and 30% of its present efficiency, there would still be sufficient capacity for the necessary German military traffic. Superimposed on this there would then come the tactical bombing after D day. In spite of this he was convinced the Germans would still continue to get a small amount of traffic through. The question was whether this would be enough. He pointed out that there were two sorts of movement:—

(a) The movement of formations. He thought that if the lines on which formations were moving were attacked, these might be delayed for a day or two.
(b) The flow of maintenance stores. Experience in Africa and Italy had shown that the effect on this of attacks on railway targets was not decisive. A line might be cut for a short time and the flow of stores interrupted, but it would then be repaired and the flow of stores would be resumed. Meanwhile, the fighting formations would have lived on their stocks which were built up during the good periods. He doubted whether the effect which would be achieved by the plan would sufficiently reduce the movement to have a military effect.

A.C.M. Tedder said that assuming that the J.I.C. [Joint Intelligence Committee] estimate of the amount of military traffic was generally accurate he was fully convinced that the plan would have military effect. In this connection he thought it important to remember that some economic traffic was bound to continue.

Sir A. Noble said that over the longer period the Germans would certainly have to make some provisions for the distribution of food to the French population, if only because a starving civilian population would be an embarrassment to Germany's military effort. During the first five weeks of OVERLORD, however, the Germans would have to move very little food for the French population, because last year's harvest had already been distributed and this year's would not yet require to be moved.

As regards France's contribution to the German war effort, it was estimated that this only amounted to about 10 per cent and, apart from beaxite [*sic*], which would not require much rail traffic, the movement of other goods could be suspended for some five weeks. The great bulk of the economic traffic is coal and industrial raw material. The Germans would certainly not hesitate to cut off this traffic if it was necessary in order to ensure the defeat of OVERLORD. Over the longer period, the Germans would have to make some provisions for the movement of coal inside France and for the export of Lorraine iron ore to Germany.

General Eisenhower said that in his opinion the question for decision was as follows. The first five or six weeks of OVERLORD would be a most critical period for the Allied armies and it was essential that we should take every possible step to ensure that they got ashore and stayed ashore. The greatest contribution that he could imagine the air forces making to this aim was that they should hinder enemy movement. Granted that the tactical plan would aim at achieving this after D Day, then how much easier would the task be made by a preparatory period in which all the air forces available after attacks on G.A.F. targets has been allowed for, would attack railway targets? This would reduce the over-all efficiency of the enemy railway system, canalise the traffic, destroy repair facilities and make it harder for the enemy to recover from the blows delivered in the tactical battle. If the preparatory bombing would help this task sufficiently to justify hopes that enemy movement would be hampered and delayed, then he thought that it was worth while, and, in default of any other alternative plan which would produce greater results, he thought the present one should be adopted.

General Kennedy agreed with General Eisenhower's statement of the problem. If the bombing of railway targets could delay movement of even one division in the critical period of the battle then it was worth while. What he was not sure about was whether the present plan of long drawn out bombing over such a wide area would result in delaying military movement. The feeling of the General Staff was that the attempt to reduce the efficiency of the whole Northern European railway system was too ambitious and that if it did not come off completely then the whole effort might have been wasted. In spite of the frequent and heavy attacks on railway targets in Italy there had been no significant interference with strategical movement there and he was doubtful whether we should be any more successful in France. What we should concentrate upon was the delay of enemy movement after OVERLORD had begun when the enemy, having discovered the point of assault, would move formations toward it. The General Staff felt that a less ambitious plan over a smaller area carried out shortly before D Day might be more effective in delaying the movement of these formations. He felt that the present plan was largely based on the experience and knowledge of civilian railway experts, who are accustomed to look at enemy transportation problems with the entirely different problems of this country in their minds, qualified no doubt by experience of conditions in the last war when the problems were also quite different. He suggested that the plan ought to be re-examined in consultation with those who were experts in working military railways, namely the staff of the Directorate of Transportation in the War Office.

General Eisenhower said that everything he had read had convinced him that apart from the attack on the G.A.F. the transportation plan was the only one which offered a reasonable chance of the air forces making an important contribution to the land battle during the first vital weeks of OVERLORD; in fact he did not believe that there was any other real alternative. He had not realized however that the War Office Staff had not been consulted on whether if the plan were successful it would have the desired effects on the enemy's military movement and he certainly agreed that they should examine the plan from this point of view. He realized that it would not be possible to provide an estimate in figures of the reduction in military traffic which might be achieved, but, in his opinion, it was only necessary to show that there would be *some* reduction, however small, to justify adopting the plan, provided that there was no alternative available.

Later in the meeting, *General McMullen* said he had no doubt that the examination could produce no other conclusion than that there would be *some* reduction in the enemy's military movements if the plan were put into effect. It would not be possible to estimate the size of the reduction. His main concern had been to emphasize that the enemy would undoubtedly be able to improvise railway facilities if the permanent ones were knocked out and that his essential movements would probably not be seriously embarrassed by executing the railway plan.

A.C.M. Tedder added that he would welcome advice from the Military Transportation Authorities during the execution of the plan.

Discussion then turned on whether there was any alternative plan worth consideration.

General Spaatz said that he had given his views on this in a paper which he had circulated before the meeting. This paper had proposed the attack of oil installations as an alternative to the Transportation Plan and had discussed the strategic and tactical merits of the two plans. It had reached the following conclusions:—

(a) Strategic attacks on the enemy railway system with the forces and within the time available would not affect the course of the initial battle and would not prevent the movement of German reserves from other fronts. On the other hand, the execution of the oil plan would force the enemy to decide to reduce oil consumption in anticipation of an impending shortage and consequent reduction in fighting power.

(b) Attacks on the vast European railway system could not within an acceptable length of time weaken the resistance of the enemy's armies on all fronts simultaneously. The oil plan would do this and would hasten the success of OVERLORD in the period after D Day.

(c) Attacks on railway targets would not force the German fighters into action whereas the enemy would defend oil installations to the last fighter aircraft.

The paper had therefore recommended that our policy should be to continue the destruction of the German Air Force and the industry supporting it, particularly the ball bearing industry, secondly to attack Axis oil production and finally to work out a plan for the direct tactical support of OVERLORD by the attack of communications and military installations of all kinds which would assist the initial phases of the battle.

General Anderson said that they had reached the conclusion that although U.S.ST.A.F. could not guarantee that the attacks of oil targets would have an appreciable effect during the initial stages of OVERLORD their studies showed that the Transportation Plan would also not have such an effect. On the other hand, the oil plan would have a decisive effect within a period of about six months whereas they did not think that the Transportation Plan would have a decisive effect within any measurable length of time.

C.A.S. said that the oil plan should certainly be considered and asked the M.E.W. representative what the effect of adopting the oil plan was expected to be on the German oil position.

Mr. Lawrence said that it had been calculated that if U.S.ST.A.F. completed their plan of attacking 27 oil installations within a period of three months then by the time a further three months was up the Germans would have had to institute a cut of 25% in their present military consumption. (This was assuming that they still hold the Roumanian oilfields.) What we could not estimate was how they would distribute this cut as between the various fronts. It was thought that they had large stocks in the West so that the effect need not be immediate. He thought that there would certainly be some effect noticeable in the West four or five months after the plan began to be put into effect.

C.A.S. said that this showed conclusively that the oil plan would not help OVERLORD in the first few critical weeks. It was, rather, a longer term plan which might have greater overall effects on the course of the war as a whole than the transportation plan but it would be six months before these were felt appreciably. He agreed however that the oil plan had great attractions and he thought we should seriously consider adopting it after the first crisis of OVERLORD was passed and we were firmly established on the continent. After all, the number of essential oil targets was not very great and it might be possible to hit all of them in a month or two of good summer weather. *General Eisenhower* entirely agreed that the oil plan should be considered as soon as the first critical situation in OVERLORD was passed.

General Kennedy said that the attack of certain army targets required consideration such as tank production and depots, M/T parks etc. *A.C.M. Leigh-Mallory* said that these would be looked after by the 9th Air Force and 2nd Tactical Air Force. He was collecting all possible information about such targets in France and would certainly work into his tactical plan any important targets of which the General Staff had information. *General Eisenhower* repeated that it looked as though there was no alternative to the transportation plan.

Some discussion then took place on whether the J.I.C. should be asked to examine possible alternative plans and make recommendations but it was eventually decided not to do this. *General Eisenhower* said he would welcome any comments that the J.I.C. cared to make on the transportation plan or on any other subject related to OVERLORD.

Consideration then turned to the tactical questions involved in using the strategic bomber force in the transportation plan.

A.C.M. Harris said that Bomber Command could contribute in two ways:—

(a) By carrying out precise attacks on railway centres within

"OBOE" [a technique for precision bombing at night through electronic guidance to targets] range during the moon periods. He pointed out that the plan required him to attack 26 such targets and he had so far only disposed of three or four. He felt extremely doubtful whether he would be able to complete his part of the plan during the time remaining, having regard to the limitations imposed by the requirements of adequate target marking and good weather in the particular areas in which the railway centres were located. This fact, together with the doubts about the effectiveness of the transportation plan as a whole made him ask that it should be most carefully examined before being adopted. In any case he urged strongly against the adoption of the alternative type of plan suggested by General Kennedy which would presumably require a larger number of attacks on precise targets and present him with a task which was quite beyond the capacity of his Command.

(b) By continuing his attacks on German cities which would of course have some incidental effect on the enemy's transportation system. He agreed that he would guide his attacks as far as possible over transportation targets but he warned General Eisenhower that the effect would be largely fortuitous. They might or might not be effective. He was of course anxious to continue attacking cities in eastern Germany for as long as the hours of darkness made this possible.
A.C.M. Tedder said there were good railway targets in eastern Germany.

General Eisenhower said that the Transportation Plan clearly meant very little change in the present Bomber Command programme. The more important question was whether the 8th and 15th Air Forces could achieve their part in it.

General Spaatz said that he would need to continue devoting one half of his effort in visual bombing to attacking G.A.F. targets. It was, however, essential that the other half should attack a target system which would produce at least some enemy fighter reaction, and so attrition. He was very doubtful whether the Transportation Plan would fulfill this condition. That was the primary reason why he had preferred the Oil Plan, which he was convinced would provoke constant air battles, and so constant attrition of enemy fighters.

C.A.S. said that this was to some extent begging the question; the enemy would no doubt not oppose attacks on railway centres unless he thought an all-out attack upon the whole railway system was being made. He might well start to send up his fighters as soon as he realized our intentions.

General Spaatz emphasized the importance of the location of the targets chosen. It was essential that his Air Forces should attack well into Germany to produce air fighting, and for tactical reasons some at least of the targets would have to be in the same areas as the G.A.F. targets.

A.C.M. Tedder entirely agreed. He said that among the crucial railway targets were the four marshalling yards on the eastern side of the Ruhr and he was confident that there was an adequate number of targets which would fit in with General Spaatz's tactical requirements.

C.A.S. asked if General Spaatz could get through his share of the Transportation Plan in the time available.

General Spaatz said this had not been worked out and *A.C.M. Leigh-Mallory* said that on the latest list of targets, there would be about 28 targets allotted to U.S.ST.A.F.

C.A.S. said that it was essential that we should know whether U.S.ST.A.F could do their share of the plan, and asked A.C.M. Tedder to tell General Spaatz what his requirements were under the plan. He thought that General Spaatz and A.C.M. Tedder should also assess whether the combination of the Transportation Plan with the attacks of the G.A.F. would produce sufficient air fighting to cause the necessary attrition. He was convinced that the attacks on G.A.F. targets would in themselves achieve this.

C.A.S. asked whether the bombing effects of the Transportation Plan would prejudice our subsequent operations on the ground in the OVERLORD area. *General Eisenhower* said that we ought not to allow this consideration to influence us at all since the Germans would certainly destroy all railway facilities as they retreated.

C.A.S. then mentioned the fact that the full execution of the Railway Plan would mean attacking a number of targets in built-up areas, and that there could not fail to be a very large number of

French civilian casualties. This was naturally a matter of some concern to H.M.G. and the Cabinet ought to be given an opportunity to consider the implications. He felt that the best solution would probably be to make a public announcement that everyone living within say one mile from any railway centre in North France was in danger and should immediately move out.

General Eisenhower and *C.A.S.* summed up the discussion, and it was decided that the following action should be taken:—

(i) A.C.M. Tedder should supply General Spaatz with the latest information about the contribution that U.S.ST.A.F. could make to the Transportation Plan. General Spaatz would then consider whether this could be achieved with half the effort of visual bombing which could be expected from the 8th and 15th Air Forces in the period available, and in conjunction with the attacks on the G.A.F., was likely to have on G.A.F. tactics and on the attrition that would be caused. The results should be reported to General Eisenhower.

(ii) A.C.M. Tedder would produce a draft directive to the Commanders concerned with the execution of the Transportation Plan, after taking into account any points that emerged in the investigation referred to in (i) above. This would be discussed with the authorities concerned and then referred to General Eisenhower. Finally, General Eisenhower and C.A.S. would discuss the matter again in a few days' time in order to reach a final decision and agree upon the directive.

(iii) A.C.M. Tedder would keep in touch with the General Staff and in particular with the military transportation experts during the execution of the plan and would immediately consider any advice that they wished to offer.

Appendix B.
The EOU Doctrine: Four Memoranda

[*Note*: The four EOU memoranda included in this appendix reflect different aspects of the doctrine evolved by the unit in 1942–1943. The first, by William Salant, addresses in general the criteria for target selection; the second and third examine certain timing factors relating to target selection; the fourth, written by me within the Air Ministry, reflects our common rather dim view of the possibilities of ending the war by lowering morale among the German populace as a whole via area bombing.]

Memorandum to EOU   17 December 1942

THE SELECTION OF INDUSTRIAL BOMBING TARGETS: SOME ANALYTICAL NOTES

A. *Introduction*

These notes deal with some analytical problems which arise in the task of assigning an order of priority to industrial targets. They are designed only as working notes for our own use, and to influence our own thinking on the subject. It is not suggested that any of the content of these notes should appear in work produced by our unit for outside use, or even that the solution tentatively suggested should be adopted in our finished work.

It is suggested, however, that this and similar discussions should influence the form of our work, just as the skeleton, though itself unseen, affects the external appearance of the body. Thus these notes are to be regarded as raw material which loses its identity in the finished product, although it plays a part in the process of manufacture.

B. *Nature of the Problem*

It is generally recognized that a large number of factors must be considered in the selection of industrial plants as targets for bombing attack. Without attempting to cover the field, we may list certain of the criteria which have been suggested:

1. *Importance of Product to War Production.* It is better to attack a factory producing something important to the war effort than one engaged in inessential output (e.g. aircraft rather than pianos).

2. *Specialization of Use Pattern.* It is better to attack a factory producing something the entire output of which goes into essential uses than one which has a wide variety of uses, varying in importance (e.g. armor plate rather than steel ingots).

3. *Importance of Individual Plant.* It is better to knock out a big plant in a given industry than a little one.

4. *Importance of Indirect Effect.* It is better to attack a factory the loss of whose output will have widespread effect in causing stoppages elsewhere than one which is a relatively isolated unit in the industrial system (other factors being equal).

5. *Tightness of Supply Situation.* It is better to attack at bottleneck points in the industrial structure than at points where there is a surplus capacity or abundant supplies.

6. *Ease of Repair.* It is better to attack plants which, if damaged, take a long time to repair or replace than those that are easily repaired.

7. *Possibility of Substitution.* It is better to attack production of a material that is essential than one for which substitutes can be found.

Other factors are:

8. *Vulnerability of Plant* to (a) high explosive; (b) fire.
9. *Size of Target.*
10. *Ease of locating Target.*
11. *Strength of Defenses at Target and En Route.* Each of these factors is a very real one which must be considered, and there are others that are not included in the list. But if a choice is to be made

between alternative targets, or a list of possible targets is to be arranged in order of priority, how can all of them be considered simultaneously, and balanced against each other? Is an essential but inaccessible Diesel engine factory a better target than a small but easily located steel mill? Assuming that each of the individual factors could be measured, how reduce the apples and pears to commensurable units?

C. *Complex Relation of the Relevant Factors*

One fairly obvious answer is that a list of all the relevant criteria should be made, and each target assigned to score (e.g. a number from 0 to 10) for each factor. The scores for a given target would be totaled and the targets could then be compared.

Unfortunately, this simple procedure is completely invalid. The various factors do not bear a simple additive relation to each other, such as is implied by adding up the separate scores to find the total for each target.

Instead, they operate at a number of different levels and their functional relations are complex. It is the purpose of these notes to elaborate difficulties, and to indicate the lines along which a solution must be found.

First, to show that there is no simple additive relation, it is obvious that a target must meet the following tests:

1. You must be able to reach it and drop bombs on it.
2. You must be able to damage it when you do hit it.
3. You must be able to impair the war effort, directly or indirectly, when you damage it.

No matter how well a target is rated on any two of these tests, if it gets a mark of zero on the third, it immediately drops out of the picture. Therefore, these criteria are not additive. Rather, they are like links in a chain.

To cite another example which has nothing to do with vulnerability or operations: It is easy to imagine a material which is used entirely for direct military purposes, whose supply cannot be expanded, but for which a satisfactory substitute is readily available. Because of the possibility of easy substitution this industry would have to be discarded as a potential target, no matter how good a showing it makes on other counts. Here again, the lack of a single link breaks the chain.

But there are other factors which do not bear a chain-like relation to each other. Two tests or criteria may be alternatives. Vulnerability to explosives and vulnerability to incendiaries are an example. If a particular plant is very vulnerable to explosives, it makes little difference whether it is or not moderately subject to damage by incendiaries, since it will be better to drop explosives in any case. (This example is not well chosen, since explosive and fire reinforce each other, so that [it] is probably desirable to use both. Thus the relations are more complex than indicated.) These two criteria are alternatives; one or the other is needed; but if one is present, the other is superfluous.

Finally, some factors are truly additive. The destruction of a given plant may reduce output of submarines, thereby affecting military production, and in addition, industrial equipment, which is classified as non-military. Probably there are many other kinds of functional relations that might be suggested.

D. *A Possible Approach*

All of the foregoing is designed to show that the relations between the many variables are complex. What bearing does this fact have on the task of target selection?

First it means that it is not enough to have a list of the variables. It is necessary also to know the general pattern of their interrelations. This knowledge need not be set out in a formal manner; it can be intuitive. But if the task of selection is divided between several groups, each handling a different part of the problem, it is desirable that some of them should be aware of the interrelations.

Second, it means that the variables should be arranged and grouped in accordance with their inter-relations, so that one can see which factors are additive, which alternative, and which are independent links. It is suggested that the following broad division of the problem into three sub-questions represents a convenient first stage in the grouping:

1. Will damage to the target hurt the enemy?
2. Can you damage it if you hit it?
3. Can you hit it, and at what cost?

These three questions are exhaustive, in that they comprise, between them, the entire problem. They are independent, in the sense that there is no overlapping. But many other sub-divisions of the problem could be made which would meet these tests. It is suggested that the advantage of this one is that different kinds of information are required to answer the questions in each group. Thus a possible division of labor is suggested. The answer to the first question requires a knowledge of the enemy's industrial structure and of his requirements for different kinds of output. It is best answered by economists, with the aid of some technical advice on strategic and tactical requirements.

The second question, as to physical vulnerability of the plant if hit, involves technical and engineering considerations relating to plant lay-out, vulnerability of different kinds of machinery and structure, etc.

The third question—can you hit the target—involves questions of the sort usually described as operational (size of target, whether easily located, strength of defenses, etc.).

For the sake of simplicity, the three questions above have been framed in qualitative terms, but it is obvious that they must be asked and answered quantitatively. The following quantitative formulation is tentatively suggested:

1. How great is the impairment of the enemy's efforts per unit of physical destruction?

2. How many units of physical destruction will be achieved per ton of bombs dropped on the target?

3. How many tons of bombs can be dropped per unit of air effort, or per unit of cost? (Including losses and wastage of planes and crew, expenditure of bombs and gasoline, etc. Analytically, it seems best to assume that virtually any objective can be achieved if sufficient effort is expended. Greater effort—in terms of sorties—will mean higher cost—however measured. Therefore cost in some sense seems to be the relevant concept.)

When combined, the answers to these three sub-questions will yield for each target the answer to the question: How much harm can be inflicted on the enemy per unit of cost to us? This final answer is obtained by multiplication of the three sub-answers as is shown when they are put in the form of ratios:

$$\frac{\text{Impairment to enemy}}{\text{Physical damage}} \times \frac{\text{Physical damage}}{\text{Tonnage of bombs}} \times \frac{\text{Tonnage of bombs}}{\text{Cost to us}} = \frac{\text{Impairment to enemy}}{\text{Cost to us}}$$

The factors "physical damage" and "tonnage of bomb hits" cancel out, leaving the ratio of "impairment of the enemy's effort" to "cost to us." Given this final result, a number of possible targets can be arranged in order of priority.

The quantitative formulation immediately raises the question of units of measurement. The measure of physical destruction used is only a matter of convenience, since physical destruction cancels out of the final equation anyway. It is necessary only that the same measure should be used in the answers to questions (1) and (2), whether it be value of plant and equipment destroyed, man-hours of labor lost (in the plant hit), or value of output lost (in the plant hit only).

A more difficult and more important problem is the measurement of impairment of the enemy's war effort. Here it seems likely that some arbitrary index must be set up if an answer in quantitative form is to be obtained. (Or the problem can arbitrarily be limited by setting a more specific objective—such as injury to the enemy's air strength, instead of impairment of his effort.)

Incidentally, it is at this point that the vital matter of timing might be introduced. Impairment of the enemy's effort three months hence might be weighted more heavily than impairment which is not felt for a year.

The first sub-question, which involves appraising the damage to the enemy's war effort resulting from given physical destruction, subsumes a large number of subsidiary questions which bear complex relations to each other, and which must therefore be appropriately handled. This group of problems might be discussed in a subsequent memorandum.

As stated at the outset, it is not suggested that our results should take the form suggested here. In particular, it is not suggested that the questions will in practice be answered in quantitative terms. It is only suggested that this analysis, or some equivalent should be in the backs of our minds.

William A. Salant

E.O.U. **Special Report No. 8**   March 9th, 1943

SELECTION OF BOMBING TARGETS
Significance of Production, Wastage, and Military Strength Ratios

Introductory Summary

1. Strength in any armament item may be regarded as a pool which is being constantly depleted by current outflow (wastage) and replenished by current inflow (production and repair). Strength is being maintained when the inflow through production and repair is just equal to the outflow through wastage.

2. If the item is quick-moving, the inflow and outflow in a month bear a high ratio to the size of the pool. This situation is typified by aircraft, where monthly production of combat types is more than one-fourth of first-line strength; repair output raises the ratio.

3. In the case of durable items, the ratios of monthly production and wastage to strength are low. Submarines are the most important item in this category, though the production-strength ratio is several times higher than the wastage-strength because the fleet is growing rapidly.

4. Action by the United Nations to reduce the German strength in these items takes two forms; diminishing the inflow of new production, and accelerating outflow through wastage.

5. There is a strong prima facie case for concentrating our efforts on diminishing the production of quick-moving items like aircraft, and on increasing the wastage of durable ones like submarines.

Attack on Aircraft

We can increase German aircraft losses through the activity of our own air forces in destroying German planes in the air and on the ground. If we are able to engage the G.A.F. heavily, as we are now doing in the Mediterranean, and as the Russians have done, we can inflict heavy enough losses to reduce German air strength by a substantial amount in a short time.

But, if it is easy to deplete an opposing air force once you can engage it, it is correspondingly difficult to keep its strength down. Because of the high ratio of current production to first-line strength, a relatively brief breathing-spell will allow a remarkable comeback. If recuperation is to be prevented engagement by our air forces must be heavy and sustained.

Our success in bringing the G.A.F. to battle is only partially under our own control. The failure of the R.A.F. to engage the G.A.F. in western Europe illustrates this fact. On the Eastern and Mediterranean fronts, air activity is associated with land warfare, and in the West, the greatest show of G.A.F. activity was evoked by the Dieppe raid. To keep German air strength down to a low level solely by shooting down German planes may prove to be impossible without resort to such costly expedients as a succession of Dieppes.

No such difficulty attends constriction of the flow of aircraft production. A substantial decline in production over a long period would have important results. To put the matter baldly, if the entire G.A.F. were knocked out of the air, the loss would eliminate the equivalent of only 4 months' production; and conversely the loss of 4 months' production is equivalent to the entire first-line strength.

Attack on Submarines

The contrast with submarines is clear. Monthly production is equivalent to only 6–8 per cent of submarines strength. There is, therefore, much greater scope for reducing strength by increasing wastage (or by immobilizing the fleet in various ways) than by curtailing production. If the entire fleet were sunk, 12 or 15 months would be required to replace it, as against 4 in the case of the air force. The loss of 4 months' production, which is equivalent to the whole of aircraft strength, represents only one-third or one-fourth of submarine strength (and, in addition, the effects on the active fleet are long delayed).

These considerations suggest that the bulk of our anti-submarine effort should seek to raise the rate of sinkings rather than to decrease the rate of production, because potentially larger dividends lie in that direction.

Since our ultimate objective is not to cut down German submarine strength, but to reduce the losses inflicted by subs on our own shipping, it is just as important to reduce the effectiveness of the submarine fleet as to cut down its numbers. In practice, these two ends are indistinguishable, since defense measures like the provision of escort vessels and anti-submarine patrols from the air are designed both to sink the submarine and to drive them away.

Efforts to raise the rate of submarine sinkings (and otherwise to reduce the effectiveness of the existing fleet) include the construction of escort vessels, improved methods of anti-submarine patrol and protection, and perhaps air attack against sub-bases (but not building yards).

In the case of aircraft, on the other hand, the division of effort between attack on production facilities designed to constrict the inflow of replacements and attack on the air force designed to increase attrition would be much more heavily weighted in favor of production.

Other Considerations

It is scarcely necessary to add that the division of effort between attack on production and attack on existing strength cannot be determined exclusively by the consideration dealt with in this report—the ratio of monthly production and wastage to strength. These ratios merely set the limits to potential accomplishments, if production is reduced to zero, and if wastage is raised to the maximum. Actual results are determined by the range of factors that may be grouped under the head "vulnerability."

But it may be noted that in the case on which attention has been concentrated, that of submarine and aircraft, consideration of vulnerability probably would not alter the conclusion that the major part of our anti-submarine effort should be concentrated against the submarine fleet, while a considerably greater part of our effort against the G.A.F. should be directed against production.

E.O.U. Special Report No. 9　　　　　　　　　　6 April 1943

TIMING OF CONSEQUENCES OF A BOMBING PROGRAM

1. In his directive to the COA, General Arnold asked the Committee to indicate the relation between the timing of a bombing program and the optimum moment for invasion of the Continent. The Committee did not reply directly to this injunction, but pointed out that the issue largely hinged on the size and effectiveness of the daylight bomber force operating from this theater.

2. While it is true that the success of any program will depend on the size and effectiveness of the daylight bomber force available, it is, nevertheless, possible to indicate certain relations between a strategic bombing and the timing of invasion.

3. The aim of the daylight bombing program, as at present conceived, is to cut down German strength in the field by diminishing current production of finished armaments. The rate at which field strength will be diminished will depend on the rates of wastage suffered by various types of armaments in relation to total field strength. Wastage will, of course, vary with German military policy and with the pressure imposed on the Germans in the field by Allied forces. But the typical relation between field strength and wastage is roughly indicated in the following table:

Armament Type (1)	First Line Strength (2)	Monthly Production (3)	Monthly Wastage (4)	Turn-over Time (2/4) (5)
Operational Aircraft	5,000	1,300	1,300	4 months
Fighters	2,000	650	650	3 months
Bombers	2,400	550	550	4 months
Submarines	300	22	6	50 months
Tanks	10,000	1,000	1,000	10 months
Army Trucks	400,000	6,000	8,000	50 months

This table shows clearly that aircraft field strength is more promptly susceptible to strategic bombing attack than any other category of German armament; and, more generally, that the effect of successful attack on armament production will be to impose a gradual wasting on German field strength, with the burden unequally borne by the various types of armament.

4. Even if one were to confine attacks to the final assembly stage of finished armaments, then, a time period would have to be allowed—varying from case to case—before the effects would be appreciably felt on field strength. The need for making a time allowance is re-enforced as one moves back, among potential targets, from the level of final assembly.

The most attractive target groups, for general attack on war production, are, it is now widely agreed, to be found in the range of components: bearings, the Bosch line, tires, and the other familiar items. It is clear that a time interval will elapse between the moment of attack and the moment when production of finished armament will be cut down for lack of the component which has been attacked. For bearings, piston rings, magnetos, and similar components, the interval will be, roughly, between two and four months for all items except trucks, where the interval is a month or less.

5. There is still another interval that must be taken into account. A time lag exists between the completion of an item of armament at the factory, and its entrance into first line strength. This interval is as short as one month for aircraft; about two months for motor trucks and tanks; at least four months for submarines.

6. Assuming that bearing production for military purposes is completely stopped by air attack, and that current rates of wastage in the field are steadily imposed on the Germans, the following table emerges by bringing together these intervals:

Ball Bearings	Months to Completion of Armament	Months to First Line Use	Months to 50% Reduction in First Line Strength
Fighter Aircraft	2½	3½	5
Bomber Aircraft	2½	3½	5½
Submarines	4	8	54
Tanks	2	4	9
Motor Trucks (light)	½	2½	27½
Motor Trucks (heavy)	1	3	28

A similar time pattern would exist for the other components which are potential targets.

7. Thus, in reply to General Arnold's query, it is of obvious importance to carry out a concerted attack on one of the major components as long before an invasion of the Continent as is possible. Even making the optimistic assumptions above, fully 5 months would elapse between the ending of bearing production and the

reduction of first line fighter strength by 50%. For tanks, it will be noted, the figure is 9 months, while no decisive effect on field strength in other categories is to be expected by bombing attacks of this kind, within reasonably short periods.

Wing Commander Burgess, A.I.3(c)2.   November 14, 1943

1. I have read with interest the paper Allied Air Attacks and German Morale. The following are comments on the evidence, the conclusions drawn in the paper, and the conclusions you would draw from the evidence for the future use of Allied air strength.

2. The evidence, most of which is familiar from the weekly reports in A.M.W.I.S. [Air Ministry Weekly Intelligence Summary], falls into two parts:

(a) evidence of increased disruption of civilian life, due to the increased weight and concentration of area attacks; and

(b) evidence with respect to the political response of the people and the government to the attacks.

3. The first type of evidence clearly shows, as stated, that the scale of casualties, evacuation, and generalized production effects have increased with the scale of attack. It should be noted, however, that almost without exception the evidence is drawn from the period immediately after a raid; and a major lesson of both British and German experience is that the discontinuity of attack gives opportunity for the application of relief and repressive measures that can re-establish order and more or less coherent social life in fairly short order.

4. The second type of evidence shows that certain weaknesses in the social and political structure of Germany have been exacerbated, notably the following:

(a) the waning popularity of Hitler and the government, due previously to the failure in Russia and defeat in the Mediterranean;

(b) the potentially disruptive presence of the mass of foreign dissident workers;

(c) the increasingly vocal desire of the German people for peace, and the somewhat increased willingness of groups of Germans to risk popular demonstration of disaffection.

5. From evidence of this type I gather that you conclude that it is within the capabilities of our air forces, in the full setting of the German military position during the next six weeks, to cause by an intensification of area raids a total collapse of the German political structure and the acceptance of defeat. You would go, then, considerably further than the negatively stated conclusion (iii) on Page 13 [of "Allied Air Attacks and German Morale"].

6. On the basis of the evidence available, and of our knowledge of the structure of the German government, and its capabilities with respect to the maintenance of order at home and in Occupied Territories, I regard that conclusion as unjustified:

(a) With respect to our capabilities, I do not believe we could create social catastrophe in a sufficient number of cities within the narrow span of time required for cumulative effectiveness to enlarge local disasters into national disruption. In this context, the case of Hamburg, which tactically was uniquely situated for this type of attack, is informative. Despite maximum effectiveness, concentration, and continuity and minimum operational losses, the Germans proved capable of coping with the situation, despite the deep and permanent impression made. Because of its location, size and the structure of its buildings, Berlin is a very much less attractive target. It is my private view that the rest of Germany would take some modest pleasure in Berlin getting it; and undoubtedly, provision has already been made for the dispersal of administrative centres.

(b) If the German leaders choose to continue the war, there is no reason to believe that they will be incapable of mustering sufficient agencies of relief and repression to avoid a general loss of control over the population. They have proved capable of maintaining control and productive activity in Northern Italy and France, against almost single-minded opposition. No evidence or argument is offered in the paper to show why area bombing, even on the scale envisaged, will cause anarchy or revolution; and there is good reason to believe that the German leaders are governing their view of the war on almost purely military considerations and would prefer, like the British leaders of 1940–41, that the air superiority mounted against them be dissipated in attacks on cities than against special targets of direct and immediate importance to the war effort.

7. It may be of interest to you that, at an early stage of work on targets, we examined from official German papers the history of collapse in 1918. It was concluded that the collapse came when Ludendorff and others saw clearly that they were defeated in the field, and that their manpower and material resources would, in a finite time, be inadequate to hold any fixed front. These were the operative considerations, not morale, and at a time when a vocal parliamentary peace party was countenanced, when internal controls were childishly lax by present standards, when the Fourteen Points offered the bulk of the population an easy way out, and the food situation was very serious indeed. I believe that collapse will come this time also from the top, and as a result of the military and military supply situation literally defined. I see no evidence or reason to believe that area bombing, whatever its great virtues as a generalised drain on the structure of Germany and its military potential, is capable of precipitating a decisive crisis.

W. W. Rostow
1st Lieutenant

As a postscript to these contemporary memoranda, the following succinct observation by Harold J. Barnett, incorporated in a letter of September 23, 1980, commenting on an earlier draft of this book, is relevant: "The Zuckerman/Tedder bias was not unrelated to area bombing bias and its underpinnings. If benefit to Allies is equated to loss to Germans, if loss to them is capital destruction, and if one thinks of total benefit to us per bomb expended by us (rather than marginal relations)—then area bombing and marshalling yards make sense. On the other hand, the EOU bias derives from contrary premises: our defining benefit to be reduction of enemy first line power; defining power in relation to the forthcoming ground context; and our use of marginal analysis, directly or indirectly."

Appendix C.

Spaatz-Eisenhower Memorandum of March 31, 1944

[*Note*: This Spaatz memorandum, written less than a week after his defeat of March 25, laid the basis for the April 5 attack on Ploești. The original carries the notation: "To A C M Tedder—Please advise, DE."]

March 31, 1944

SUBJECT: Use of Strategic Bombers in Support of OVERLORD

TO : General Dwight D. Eisenhower

1. It is accepted that the attack of the GAF (and Ball Bearings) and railroads in France are prerequisites to the success of OVERLORD.

2. No conclusive answer has been advanced as yet, however, to the question: "In supplementation of the attack of railroads in France and the GAF, will the attack of railroads in Germany or oil in Germany have the most effect upon OVERLORD?"

3. The Rail Experts state that, at best, the attack of a few of the hundreds of rail targets *in Germany* will have only a very limited effect upon the movements against OVERLORD. At the same time, the effect of attacks on oil is considered to be difficult to determine as to time of impact, and hence indefinite as far as effect on the early stages of OVERLORD is concerned. There is, therefore, no quantitative measure of the effect of *either*, although the fact that the rail attack will have *some* effect in time is more apparent. That

does not preclude an effect from the oil attack, however, of which there is a good chance in view of the known present fuel tightness.

The effect from the oil attack, while offering a less definite impact in time, is certain to be more far-reaching. It will lead directly to sure disaster for Germany. The rail attack can lead to harassment only.

4. In weighing these two, it appears that too great a price may be paid merely for a certainty of a very little. This is especially true in view of:

 a. The possibility of increasing the available effort through:

  (1) Use of Eighth Air Force Fighter Bombers in attacks against French railroad targets.

  (2) Use of RAF Bomber Command in daylight attacks against French railroad targets.

  (3) Use of Eighth Air Force Fighter Bombers in attacks against the Synthetic Plants in the Ruhr.

  (4) Use of RAF Bomber Command in attack against Synthetic Plant at Stettin and possibly the Ruhr.

 b. The possibility of interdicting the transportation lines in the Roumanian area.

 c. The possibility that the Russians will either secure Ploesti or bring it within range of their light air units.

5. The interdiction of the transportation lines about Ploesti would serve a four-fold purpose: It would hamper German ground operations in the area, reduce the flow of refined products from Ploesti, restrict the flow of crude to refineries outside that area, and contribute to the general dislocation of the German rail system. If Ploesti should be taken or neutralized, that would justify attacks upon the synthetic plants in Germany in preference to any other targets, for they would then become almost the sole source of refined products. These possibilities, therefore, lend weight to the advantages of early attack upon the Synthetics in order to obtain the earliest possible impact. That impact might well be far earlier than currently estimated.

6. In view of the above, and of the great extent to which attack on rail transportation and motor fuel supplement one another, recommend that, for the present, priority for attacks by USSTAF be given to:

a. For the Eighth Air Force:
    (1) GAF and Ball Bearings.
    (2) Rail transportation targets (19) in occupied countries.
    (3) Synthetic Oil Plants (13).
  b. For the Fifteenth Air Force:
    (1) GAF and Ball Bearings.
    (2) Rail transportation in Roumanian area and selected targets in southern France.
    (3) Synthetic plants in southeast Germany.
    (4) Political targets in the Balkans.
7. An identical letter has been furnished to Sir Charles Portal, Marshal of the Royal Air Force.

>CARL SPAATZ
>Lieutenant General, USA
>Commanding

Appendix D.

Report on the May 7, 1944, Destruction of the Bridge at Vernon

[*Note*: As paragraph 1 suggests, this report was evoked by the excitement in London following the success of the Vernon bridge attack of May 7. It is one of many documents in the Air Ministry and other files reflecting a greatly heightened interest in bridge bombing, including the Mediterranean experience, at that time.]

HEADQUARTERS 365th FIGHTER GROUP
OFFICE OF THE COMMANDING OFFICER
APO 595, U. S. ARMY

11 May 1944.

SUBJECT: Report on Low-Level Attack on Railway Bridge at Vernon, France.

TO : Undersecretary of State for Air, Air Ministry, Whitehall, London.
Attn: Directorate of Air Tactics.

1. In response to telephone request of 10 May 1944, the following report of destruction of railway bridge at Vernon, France, is herewith submitted.

Narrative of Operation

On 7 May 1944 at 1146 hours, the group formation made L/F [landfall] in at Fecamp, France, at 12,000 feet. The weather at this time was roughly 8/10 [cloud cover], clouds at 3000–7000 feet. An occasional glimpse was caught of the ground, and the formation was thus able to remain oriented. There were two assigned targets and the group was briefed for "A" Force to attack the steel bridge at Vernon and "B" Force the two concrete bridges at Mantes-Gassicourt.

At 1157 hours, "B" Force (12 P-47 bombers with escort) broke away and proceeded on course. Vernon was located through a break in the overcast, and the striking force (12 P-47 bombers and escort) orbited in the immediate vicinity.

Technique of attack, as briefed, consisted of individual low-level, point blank range attacks at 30 second interval on abutment supporting north end of the bridge. Two 1000 lb G.P. [general purpose] bombs, 8–11 second delay, were to be utilized. It had been decided to concentrate attacks on one point only, due to the proximity of an ammunition factory a few hundred yards north of bridge. Therefore, a single approach path was determined upon to avoid the factory on both approach and withdrawal.

While the force orbited at 10,000 feet above the break in the overcast, the first man initiated the attack on the target. He dove for the deck south of Vernon, leveled out over the town and drove straight for north abutment at deck level and full throttle. His flight path was about 25 degrees off axis of bridge and point of aim was intersection of bridge and foundation supporting north end of the steel span. The bombs were released at point blank range and he pulled up over the bridge, breaking left with evasive maneuvers on the deck. Some miles west of the target, he zoomed up as briefed, entered the overcast and made rendezvous with escorting fighters on top.

The leader "S-ed" behind the first plane to give himself a 30 second interval, and delivered the same attack. He pulled up and remained under the overcast to direct the attack and observe results. During the attack, the bombers were the target of the most intense light flak they have yet encountered. Although there was a flight of escort fighters standing by to strafe flak towers, it was decided not to use them because the fire seemed to come from all directions, and it was not believed that strafing the general area was worth the additional risk of subjecting these planes to unnecessary fire.

The remaining bombers were then called and brought down through the overcast individually. The bombing results were excellent and as the smoke cleared away from the sixth attack, the north end of the bridge collapsed into the water. The remaining flight was immediately ordered to strike the alternate target, the ammunition factory north of the bridge. Two planes were already committed to the attack however, so they were ordered to hit the center bridge support, which they did with such effectiveness, that the entire north span collapsed and crashed into the water, thus paralyzing not only rail transportation but probably water transportation as well. The attack on the factory was delivered with very good results. A glide bombing technique was utilized bombing under cloud cover at altitudes varying from 1000–1600 feet. This almost proved disastrous as the bombs set off a sympathetic detonation immediately, and the whole building blew up. Two aircraft were severely damaged at 1600 feet by concrete blocks and barely managed to reach home. The explosion threw debris to an altitude of at least 3000 feet.

Two aircraft failed to return from the mission, both planes being hit by flak over the target, as they were making their bomb run; one chute was seen to open, and the other pilot is believed to have bailed out. Five other P-47's were badly damaged.

The formation made L/F out as briefed landing at base at 1338 hours.

(Sgd.) LANCE CALL,
Colonel, Air Corps,
Commanding.

G. 20224.

Appendix E.

Bombing Policy on the Eve of the Battle of the Bulge: Memorandum of W. W. Rostow, December 6, 1944

[*Note*: I wrote this memorandum on December 6, 1944, ten days before the Battle of the Bulge began. As a working member of the Air Ministry, I addressed it to the senior U.S. liaison officer to Air Ministry Intelligence as well as to Hughes. I forwarded a copy to Kindleberger at Bradley's headquarters in France. It reflects dissatisfaction with the September–December 1944 diffusion of bombing effort even before Rundstedt's forces struck early on Saturday morning, December 16.]

Col. Kingman Douglass
Col. R. D. Hughes

1. At the present time the bomber forces are devoting the bulk of their effort to railway and area targets. These are strategic targets of long run attrition, tempered with occasional tactical bonuses in the form of German troop casualties, damage to barracks, ammunition trains, and other random bystanders.

2. These objectives have been accepted in preference to targets of greater real military content for a variety of reasons:
   (a) because of the alleged complementary character of railway and oil attacks;
   (b) because, like a carrot, a short term view of the war has been held before the air forces, and the western railway

centers were speciously argued to constitute short run targets;

(c) because operational conditions made impossible all but occasional visual attacks, and railway-area targets are suitable to our present blunted capabilities.

3. By the end of this month it appears probable that an additional 5–6 months of European War will be frankly accepted. And from January some progressive improvement in the weather is likely.

4. It is, therefore, suggested as urgent that the bomber forces formulate a program for the final phase of the European War. Without a positive program, carefully considered in the light of the probable ground force sequence, it is likely that we will end the war in a blaze of mediocrity; for, from the beginning the transport attacks have appealed as an easy way of filling the vacuum, without planning, without exploiting the intelligence, without thinking through our full capabilities.

5. The period (say) January 1–June 1, 1945, will probably fall into two phases: the period of relative quiescence and build-up, running perhaps to sometime in April; and the final push. It will be agreed that oil and the containing of the Me.262 [the first operational jet-propelled fighter], if the latter is judged necessary, are continuing first priority objectives for the first phase. The balance of visual effort should then be returned to ordnance depots, tank, and M/T [motor transport] factories and sources of other military equipment may present useful targets which should be explored in military intelligence. This will be a period of build-up for the enemy as well as for ourselves, and the time periods estimated involved, if correct, would make winter production relevant to the spring battle.

6. In this period intensive study should be given to two problems:
   (a) close support;
   (b) interdiction.

7. There can be little doubt that the close support operations thus far carried out have indicated considerable promise; but they represent, perhaps inevitably, immature first ventures. In particular, every effort must be made to guarantee a quick follow up on the ground; aiming points must be chosen in conformity with the actual needs of the spear-head ground force units and after intimate

consultation at the level of those units; a system of intelligence and planning must be set-up to permit a sequence of such operations flexibly to follow the changing pattern on the ground.

8. The strategic and tactical transport operations since Normandy have constituted merely random attrition. This has been partly caused by the admitted difficulties of imposing interdiction on the multiple lines of western Germany; but there has been a notable lack of an over-all plan, with consequent anarchy in the tactical air force transport operations.

9. Interdiction has been proved in the Mediterranean and in the West a formidable military weapon against an army engaged in active fighting. As in other air operations it has been shown that the completion of a system yields benefits greater than the sum of particular damage inflicted. There can be little doubt that the enemy could be denied rail transport for a distance up to 100 miles behind the front with the air forces now available to the task. Multiple line cuts regularly policed could achieve this end, if sufficient operationally feasible rail bridges are not available. Some such transport target system, designed to hollow the enemy's resilience once engaged, must be sought.

10. Once the final battle is joined the air forces must be prepared with a dual program of interdiction and close support, fitted to the real and immediate needs of the ground forces. Planning similar to that which preceded D-day will be required.

11. It may be argued that it is up to the ground forces to formulate the time periods and to suggest appropriate targets for each. In fact they have proved incapable of setting an appropriate air plan; and, since the strategic bomber forces defaulted so far as a positive plan was concerned, the advocates of rail centers—strongly placed, but equally out of touch with the details of the ground force problem and air force capabilities, under good planning—pushed through on every past occasion. There can be little doubt that they will do so again, and that in consequence the bomber forces will continue to be misused. It will do us little credit if we do not make a serious effort to avoid repeating the errors of March–April, 1944.

W. W. Rostow, Capt.

6. 12. 44.

Appendix F.

German Rail Movement in France in the First Ten Days after D-Day: An Interim Report by Charles P. Kindleberger, June 16–19, 1944

[*Note*: This rather remarkable memorandum, written by Kindleberger as of June 19, 1944, provides a clearer picture of the German buildup after D-Day in relation to transport attacks than any of the official histories. It also illustrates the painstaking and self-critical way EOU went about its business. The memorandum reflects the continuing evaluation effort conducted at G-2 SHAEF by Robert Roosa and a British captain, Andrew Stark, who in the postwar years rose in the Foreign Office ranks to the post of ambassador.]

G (Air) Branch
21 Army Group
Headquarters, 2 TAF

19, June, 1944

SUBJECT: ATTACHED INTERIM REPORT

TO : Lt. Col. A. A. Part, GS (I)

1. Attached is a copy of an "interim" report on the rail movement of German reserves. In view of my imminent departure [for France], I fear it will have to serve as a final report as well.

2. Apologies are due you for the length, disorganization,

wretched typography, and infelicities of expression. I sorely missed my comfortable office and competent secretary.

3. I shall be grateful if you will point out the many military mistakes of interpretation. For railway lore, I am myself responsible; on the military side, I have incorporated—in order to make a more rounded document—a number of impressions, begged, borrowed, stolen and perhaps dreamt.

4. It may not be amiss to mention at this point that I have enjoyed very much the opportunity to work on this problem and with your staff during this past month.

C. P. Kindleberger
Captain, AUS

G (Air) Branch
21 Army GROUP
Headquarters, 2 TAF

16 June 1944

SUBJECT: INTERIM REPORT ON THE RAIL MOVEMENT OF GERMAN RESERVES

TO : Lt. Col. A. A. Part, GS (I)

1. The following memorandum is intended to summarize some of the impressions gained from the flow of evidence which has passed through the Tn [Transport] Section on German movement of reserves and the efficacy of various forms of Allied attack designed to impede this movement. It is written at D plus 10 in an attempt to digest some of the welter of detail before it is forced out of memory by the continued flow. It is intended to be neither exhaustive (Captain Ezra is to write an official account of the movement) nor eclectic. Indeed, it may here and there point a moral to adorn the tale.

2. In substance, the memorandum deals with our expectations regarding the move of enemy reinforcements to the battle area, the actual course of movement taken by the enemy, the pre–D-day plans designed to counter this movement, their success, and enemy reactions. Finally it points out certain lessons for continued opera-

tions, and draws certain conclusions which may be useful in the event that invasions of other continents are contemplated with the use of overwhelmingly superior air forces.

Rate of Enemy Build-Up

3. According to the Information Center, the enemy now has but 14 divisions, plus one mobile brigade in the battle. This is much below expectation, as may be judged from SHAEF figures of 25 May, set forth in a report "Effects of Recent Attacks on Rail Centers etc. . . ." This put enemy divisions in the Neptune area at:

D	3
D + 1	7
D + 3	13
D + 7	21
D + 25	26
D + 60	50

Of the 14 divisions in the battle, only 4 have travelled by rail for any considerable distance or in any considerable strength. These are 2nd Panzer from the Amiens area, possibly parts of Panzer Lehr from Chartres, parts of 17 SS Pz Gr from Thouers-Poitiers, and 3 Para. from Brittany. Currently en route are 2 more Pz formations— 2nd SS Pz, which is nearing the battle lines, and 16 Pz which was still entrained yesterday S of the Loire. CK reports have discussed movement of heavy Panzer formations—possibly Corps brigades from N. of Mailly, and of 2 separate train movements from Germany. One of the latter may be associated with another report of an infantry division entraining in Denmark. If each of these movements were scored as equivalent to a division, and each as having arrived this morning, the enemy would have succeeded in getting 19 divisions into the battle by D plus 10, as contrasted with the expectation of 21 divisions by D plus 7.

4. The writer is not competent to discuss the military reasons for this delay in enemy build-up. It may not be presumptuous, however, to suggest that the cover has worked extremely well. The enemy clearly appears to have expected us to make a series of landings—along the Bay of Biscay coast as well as in the Dieppe-Boulogne area; and has, on this account, been hesitant about throwing his reserves into the battle at the cost of emptying other areas. Some part of the credit, however, may be due the line of interdic-

tion along the Seine. With quick lateral movement across the river prevented, our maneuverability on the sea greatly exceeded his on the land. In consequence, he was obliged to keep strong forces on both sides of the river, as is illustrated by the failure of 116 Pz to enter the battle (although it is known to be a weak division) and the enemy's move in replacing 2 Pz at Amiens with 1 SS Pz after the former had been moved.

Coverage of Enemy Movement—Entraining

5. The photographic intelligence on enemy divisional movements was excellent, with the exception of the 3 Para division in Brittany. For the others, there were perhaps a few alarums which in retrospect will prove to have been misleading (and due to the expectation that the enemy would react more immediately); but the movement of elements from Chartres and Poitiers was spotted, as were the main moves from Amiens, Toulouse and Bordeaux.

Coverage of Enemy Movement—En Route

6. Tac-R, Photo-Recce, and the ALO system in effect with fighter and bomber units have worked well to give us a fairly full picture of the enemy use of French and to a lesser extent Belgian railroads. While this cover has been wide, it has not always been complete, due to weather on the one hand, and gaps which inevitably arise on the other. One of the gaps has been Paris, which probably requires photo recce because of the flak danger to low flying aircraft. Information on train movement in Brittany, far out on the peninsula, came almost exclusively from 8th AF fighters escorting bombers to Nantes and similar targets. In the Rennes, Dol, Redon area, however, the coverage was complete.

Coverage of Enemy Movement—Detraining

7. *a.* It is possible from the coverage received to give a fairly detailed picture of the detraining stations used by the enemy, although inevitably some mysteries are residual in the picture. On D Day, and for a time on D plus 1, the enemy was enabled to use the line Granville to Argentan for detraining. This was probably utilized by the elements of 17 SS Pz Gr from Thouers and Poitiers which arrived by train, whereas other elements moved the entire distance by road. After D plus 1, it is believed that the enemy was unable to use any part of this line for detraining, although it is admitted that the presence of "K" trains in Villedieu on the morning of 13 June

may argue against this, despite the fact that they were empty. Some heavy flats have been seen on the Caen-Flers line above Thury Harcourt, which probably represent wagons used in this initial movement.

 b. The movement of 2nd Pz was spread out over several days and involved the use of various detraining areas as various lines were open or blocked by bomb damage. The first elements, which may have been those which entrained at Achiet-le-Grande and Miraumont (between Albert and Amiens) on the morning of 9.6, appear to have been forced by damage at Acheres and Versailles to go south of Paris through Masey Palaiseau and Juvisy to Chartres, when they fanned out to Dreux, Maintenon, La Loupe and Courville and detrained on the evening of 9.6. Later units were able to get through the Grande Ceinture which may have been repaired, after the attack by Bomber Command of 7/8 June by the evening of 9.6. Trains getting through were unable, however, to get past blocks at Mantes Gassicourt, where the marshalling yards had been attacked by medium bombers, and so detrained at Mantes, at Meulan and at Poissy; or past Dreux because of blocks S of Evreux and east of Monancourt, so that further detraining activity took place at Dreux and at Bueil.

 c. It is not at all clear where 3 Para detrained, but the weight of the incomplete evidence points to Rennes and vicinity. Fully 12 trains of those required to carry the division were spotted in the morning of 10.6, but none of these were in the Dol, Pontoson, Avranches area, but rather at L'Hermitage (west of Rennes) and in Rennes itself. It seems likely that the division moved to the front by M/T held in parks in and about Rennes. Lack of available M/T on the lateral Avranches-Argentan may provide part of the explanation why detraining did not take place in this area, although the weight of bomb damage inflicted along this line makes such an explanation superogatory. My records do not show the state of serviceability of the Pontaubault bridge after the original attack of 7 June, but the RAF Bomber Command effort of 8/9 June cut tracks and it has since been out of commission,—now on a semi-permanent basis.

 d. Post Facto It is reasonable to relate the detraining activity at Argentan and Alencon on the first several days to Panzer Lehr from the Chartres area. It will be recalled that indications that part of this division was to entrain were seen in the activity in Chateaudun late on D day. In retrospect, it appears that the Bomber Command attack of 7/8 locked the barn after the horse was stolen. Most of the division, judging by road movement, did come on M/T.

e. We have seen no indication that 77th Inf. used trains in moving from Mont St. Michel area to the battle; nor in fact is there any record of seeing it move by road. I take it the distance favors road movement. Whether 5 Para moving from further west in Brittany used road or rail is again obscure, although some of the train movement seen on the peninsula may be attributable to it. This is not likely, however, since as already pointed out, train movement east of Jugon has been seen only on the line running southeast to La Brohiniere and Rennes, and not on the line due east to Dol.

f. The foregoing has neglected to point out that some detraining took place immediately north of the Loire, at La Fleche for example, on about D plus 4. This movement cannot be linked, so far as I know, to any particular division. That part of 2nd SS Panzer which was able to cross the Loire on the bridge at Port Boulet prior to 0730 hrs on 14.6 did, however, detrain at La Fleche, Sille le Guillaume, Sable-sur-Sarthe, and possibly Laval and Le Mans. One train which appears almost certainly to have been part of this movement was attacked successfully running east from Le Mans to Montfort, possibly in an effort to gain access to the single-track lines running north to Mortagne-au-Perche, St Gauberge, Vimoutiers and Mezidon. Blocks on the main double track lines (Rennes-Folligny, and Le Mans-Alencon-Argentan) and damage to the single track lines (Vitre-Fougeres-St. Hilaire-Vire and La Chappelle Athenaise-Mayenne-Domfront-Flers) has made these routes north from the Rennes-Le Mans lateral impossible.

g. The rest of 2nd SS Panzer seems to have detrained south of the Loire and to have pursued main roads as far as Laval, Le Mans and Chartres, and secondary roads thereafter. It is probable that 16 Pz from Bordeaux, held up yesterday by the attack on Angouleme, will also detrain south of the Loire. There is a possibility, however, that it may attempt to swing over to Vierzon and then north and west through the Orleans-Paris gap which is not yet completely blocked off.

h. Honorable mention must be given to Mezidon, which has been the enemy's most advanced detraining station capable of handling a small but continuous amount of traffic. Whether this traffic represents single trains of divisional moves or supply is not clear. It is painfully clear, however, that each noon, after attack, Mezidon is seen fairly empty and inactive, whereas about 5 o'clock in the evening it gradually expands in activity and gets full by 2000 hours. This pattern has been repeated on the 13th, 14th, and 15th. It is probable that the traffic to Mezidon, which is likely to be supplemented by detraining points at Argentan and Surdon, and may currently share traffic with Lisieux and Bernay, comes up through Mortagne-au-Perche, Ste Gauberge, Vimoutiers etc. It is possible, however, that some of the traffic originates at Honfleur or Sotteville, and represents ferrying leakages across the Seine (see below).

The Seine Blocks

8. While the barrier of the Seine has given us some uneasiness, as we watch for repairs, mistake piers for pontoons, worry about ferrying, and mistake dams for bridges, it has nonetheless been of solid benefit to the whole operation. In addition to the fact that is has forced the complicated detour through or south of Paris on troops which have moved, it has had the strategic advantage, in combination with the cover plan, of forcing the enemy to keep some considerable amount of strength north of the river. This point has already been made in para. 4 above. Two minor points about leaks may be worth noting:

a. Ferry activity on the river has been quite conspicuous, and all of us have been somewhat slow in taking note of it. I take it that it is not confirmed that the 84th Infantry Division has joined the battle. This might have crossed by ferry and by landing barge from Le Havre to Honfleur, if any organized unit has so crossed. It is, however, quite clear that considerable numbers of men and some vehicles have crossed by ferry and barge, although the numbers that can do so in the future will certainly be limited after the attacks on Le Havre, Quillebeuf, Duclair and the ferries themselves.

b. It is surprising that the Germans have not attempted more effectively to bridge the river with military type structures. There is a theory, mentioned by Captain Stark, that the pontoon emplacements at Rouen form the basis for a pontoon bridge which is erected each night and taken down each morning at first light. This seems rather unlikely; and until evidence on the point is obtained, I should be inclined to regard it as romantic. It may be worth noting, however, that a train was seen today moving south from Sotteville to the junction at Foret de la Londe. This may have some connection with military supplies getting across the river by ferry or by pontoon bridge, although the capacity of either route is certain to be very limited.

Perhaps no more eloquent statement about the value of the line of cuts along the Seine can be made than by quoting a message received from the 2nd Army on 14 June:

INFORMATION—IN LOG

File No.	Date/Time	Originator	Summary
41	131450	2 Army	Request attention Hy bombing of Seine bridges to be continued. This particularly applies to pontoons existing or under construction in order to delay arrival of reinforcements from NORTH of river. Also require latest information on situation this river.

The Loire Blocks

9. With the successful conclusion of yesterday morning's attacks against the Loire rail bridges, at a time when 16 Pz division was already moving north toward the NEPTUNE area, it is possible to take a fairly satisfied view of the course of action here. All ten bridges are out of action for at least five days, and three of these 10 are in a state to require reconstruction. This was, however, a fairly close shave. Attack was directed against the bridges first on June 8 when blocks were achieved on 4 of the 10 and slight damage inflicted on two others. Occasional attack by fighters thereafter whittled down the number of serviceable bridges until the morning of the 15th, when the last round of attacks polished off the job. During the 13th and 14th, however, at least one bridge—the single-track line at Port Boulet,—was open, and the Germans appear to have been able to run a considerable amount of traffic across it. The fact that the bulk of the division detrained south of the Loire was, in my judgement, due to the limited capacity of this route. Had one more bridge,—a double track line—been open—it is probable that

all of 2nd SS Panzers trains could have got across the river. It should be pointed out, moreover, that this division was slow in getting to the line of the Loire partly because of damage inflicted by the RAF on Poitiers, attacked on 12/13 June, and partly as a result of attacks on the rail line of the South West by resistance groups.

10. How valuable the delay to 2nd SS Panzer's grouping for participation in the battle, and undoing the wear on its vehicles and tracks which the 120 mile run imposed on it will be, I am not in a position to say. It may, however, have an effect on this week-end's push. In any event, it is clear that 16 Pz will arrive late in the battle, delayed on the one hand by the resistance groups, by the RAF attack on Poitiers, the 8th Air Force attack on Angouleme, and the necessity to proceed from the Loire by road. Some elements may succeed in detouring through the Orleans-Paris gap by rail, but the capacity of these routes is now limited, and traffic from the south must compete with that from the North and East.

The Paris-Orleans Gap

11. At the time when the proponents of attacks against bridges were still battling uphill, they included in the program of the Seine and the Loire rail bridges, 4 Paris junctions for attack every other day. This was shortsighted. For the Paris junctions have not been satisfactory for blockage: they have leaked. And it has been difficult, I take it, to have them attacked with sufficient frequency to ensure that they remained blocked. The record of their attack is as follows:

Date	Acheres	Versailles Matelots	Massy Palaiseau	Juvisy
June 2	8th AF	Cloud obscured	8th AF	8th AF
June 4	——	8th AF	8th AF	——
June 6/7	RAF BC (poor)	——	——	——
June 7	8th AF	8th AF	8th AF	8th AF
June 7/8	RAF BC	RAF BC	RAF BC	RAF BC
June 10/11	RAF BC	RAF BC	——	——

The attack of June 7, however, was carried out in heavy cloud with PPF [radar] techniques. The risk of bad weather, however, is one which must be encountered in planning any form of precisely timed air attack.

12. It has already been pointed out that trains have gotten through these junctions particularly on June 10th, when the 2nd Pz was moving through Paris to Mantes, Meulan and Poissy, and on June 14th, when a train of 50 plus oil cars seen on a siding near the junction in the morning is likely to be the same train of 50 plus oil cars seen in Dreux in the afternoon of the same day.

13. In addition to the leakage through the junctions, it must be reported that the original conception of a program of attacks against railroads was inadequate in the attention it paid to the three single track lines running between Paris and Orleans in an East-west direction. It was felt that these routes were of low capacity, involved complicated working, and could be adequately dealt with by one or two blows which would discourage the Germans from their use. This was far too optimistic. Attack against this part of the gap has involved only an RAF BC attack of 10/11 June against Etampes and one on 8 June when the 8th AF tried to destroy the Etampes junction but succeeded primarily in its other attack, against the junction at Orleans.

The Germans have succeeded in working traffic through the gap by one or more routes every day. This traffic now meets blocks on the line of bridge and embankment cuts from Mantes to Beaugency, including Cherisy, Epernon, Coltainville, Chartres and Cloyes, but it is not yet certain that this series of blocks has been effectively imposed. When these engineering structures have been destroyed, the Paris junctions and the gap between Orleans and Juvisy will have been effectively provided for, even though the line to which the enemy will be able to bring rail traffic will have moved somewhat west.

Movement inside the Area (as of 19 June, 1944)

14. While there have been a number of leaks into the area bounded by the Seine to Mantes, Chartres, Beaugency and the Loire to Nantes, one of the most remarkable features of the German use of the railways has been his ability to use them for traffic, originating within the area. It was anticipated, before the battle began, the enemy would use the rail system inside the Seine-Loire ring only if it were left relatively free of damage; and that a moderate amount of damage, even of a relatively unenduring character, would be sufficient to discourage entirely his use of a truncated rail system.

This view it appears is erroneous. Eventually, the provision of locomotive coal from NE France may prove such a difficult problem that rail traffic inside the ring is abandoned. At the moment, however, the enemy appears to be prepared to operate rail lines 20 miles behind the battle lines, even if these lines are cut so that it is impossible to bring in trains from a further distance.

15. Our error in expecting abandonment of railway facilities within the ring after a moderate amount of damage is compounded of two miscalculations. In the first place, it was not realized how acute the enemy's shortage of motor transport and petrol in fact is; secondly, it was not appreciated that a considerable haulage inside the ring is required to transport supplies from main dumps to the battle area, and that this will, if possible, be performed by rail even if transport from outside the ring to the dumps is forced on the road.

16. The evidence for the enemy's continued use of the rails is found partly in the fact that traffic appears at Mezidon, Surdon, Argentan, Lisieux, etc.—ie. forward railheads in greater amount than appears to be filtering through the outer line of cuts; partly in the time of the movement into Mezidon, which makes it appear to be a well-regulated movement of supply which differs from the characteristic troop train movement; and to a considerable extent in the fact that extensive, but superficial damage to track, junctions, embankments and marshalling yards inside the area is continuously under repair despite the increasing damage to major engineering structures—which the Germans appear to be unwilling or unable to repair, on the outer ring itself. Evidence of repair has been seen at Argentan, Mezidon, Surdon, Lisieux, Bonancourt, Dreux, Laigle, Evreux etc. Not much repair or movement has been seen on the western lateral boundary of the Continental peninsula, probably in my view because access to it has been interdicted by adequate blocks in the form of destroyed bridges (except on the two single-track lines).

17. There seems to be a distinct possibility that the enemy has used narrow gauge railways both in the area close to the battle zone and further back. The practice in the battle area, for the purpose of carrying supplies from rear to forward dumps, is of course economical, except that the haul appears to have been made for a distance of as short as 20 miles. The evidence in support

of this is the fact that 2 Group on the night of 16/17 June observed a train near the Foret de Cinglais. This appears to have been on the narrow gauge line from Falaise to Caen, which passes close to the Foret de Cinglais where dumps are located. In the more remote areas, a train of passenger cars was spotted in motion SW of Fougeres at a point on the narrow gauge line from Rennes to Fougeres. It is possible that this line was used to transport troops from Brittany which had been brought to Rennes by standard-gauge line. It is not worth spending much time watching the narrow-gauge railways; but they cannot altogether be neglected.

18. As for movement over the railways inside the ring on standard-gauge lines, it may be concluded that the enemy will continue to repair and use these lines so long as damage is readily repairable on the one hand, and so long as coal is available to run locomotives on the other. To prevent movement immediately, one can maintain superficial damage to the lines by continuous attacks against track, junctions, marshalling yards, or one can attempt to find complex engineering structures such as bridges and viaducts, which if destroyed, require little if any reattack. In actuality, the choice is not as simple as this, since some lines lack such structures. These must be kept under continual surveillance and be repeatedly attacked. Other lines, however, can be blocked for considerable periods of time by the destruction of large engineering structures, requiring reconnaissance thereafter only at fairly long intervals to determine whether repair is being undertaken.

Reconnaissance Requirements

19. In one respect, our effort has not perhaps been all that it might have been: claims of damage by wide-ranging fighter aircraft in armed recce missions have been substantiated only in a few instances by photographic reconnaissance. This gap may have been inevitable during the early stages of the invasion as reconnaissance flights were made to cover a host of potential entraining stations. It is, however, and will continue to be unsatisfactory, if fairly circumstantial claims of lasting damage cannot be substantiated by the proof afforded by photography. Three cases may be cited: on D or D plus 1, fighter aircraft claimed the destruction of small but not inconsequential railroad bridges at St. Medard-sur-Ille (on the line north from Rennes to Dol) and at Forgan on the line north from

Alencon to Argentan. The former has never been substantiated, although the absence of movement on the line ever since D plus 1 makes it appear likely that damage was in fact done to the bridge. The latter was not surveyed by reconnaissance, but a 9th Bomber Command mission 8–10 days later, dispatched against the neighboring Foret d'Ecouves, noted that the bridge was in fact destroyed. In the third place, fighter claims of the destruction of two bridges and a tunnel on the line north from Redon to Rennes have been made but no photographic evidence has been obtained to lend or detract credence to these claims.

20. It is of obvious importance to know the position of the enemy's rail lines, whether damage be inflicted in pre-planned or spontaneous attacks. Methods should be devised, in my judgment, to enable fairly circumstantial claims, winnowed from the myriad claims received after a day when all the fighters are out on armed reconnaissance to be covered photographically. Only those of importance can be covered. They should be chosen presumably by someone who has the enemy transport picture fairly well in mind. This photography will, in the case of established claims, divert preplanned missions from the affected lines, and aid in economizing effort which should evidently be directed solely against lines which the enemy is or will shortly be capable of using.

21. Further to the same point, repeat photography of established damage appears to be distributed rather inequitably. Well known lines of interdiction, like the Loire and the Seine get frequent cover. This is quite appropriate, since it is important to learn whether the enemy is making attempts to cross one river, the Seine, by ferry, barge, pontoon, or temporary bridge, and the Loire by road. Inside the ring, and outside at a considerable distance, however, follow-up photographs are obtained at most infrequent intervals. It is known that the Maintenon viaduct was destroyed in early May; cover was obtained on June 4; none has been obtained since. The uncertainty attaching to the status of the Mantes, Cherisy etc. cuts is well known to you; and steps are being taken to correct it. Our latest picture of Pontaubault—five were obtained between June 9 and 12—is now a week old, and we do not know whether the enemy has cleared up the craters in the road bridge and the eastern single-line rail bridge from St. Hilaire du Harcouet to Avranches. These instances could be multiplied. The moral is clear. Photographic

effort is now closely linked to current planned attacks and to outstanding efforts of the past. Some should be allocated to following repair and reconstruction on garden-variety attacks of the past where continued damage is useful to us, and repairs, if complete, will be useful to the enemy.

Observations

22. *Attacks on Marshalling Yards* In my view, the pre–D-day program of attacks on marshalling yards has had almost no effect on German rail movement, so far as it has been possible to observe it. You will recall my pointing out to you that the enemy has used the route Ghent, Mouscron, Lille, Arras, Amiens for one movement from Germany. Another division, possibly that from Denmark, came through the route north of Antwerp along the same line in 38 trains at the rate of 12 trains a day beginning about 14 June. Currently, moreover, it is reported that 1st SS Pz is moving by rail over 17, 18 and 19 June by rail lines Ghent, Mons, Erquelines, Aulnoye, Tergnier, Compiegne, Creil, Persan Beaumont, and Le Bourget. These routes sound like catalogues of "rail centers" which have received "A" damage and never require reattack. There is no evidence of which I am aware, that is, that the Germans have been handicapped by the "paralysis" created by attacks against locomotive servicing facilities; and the positive evidence that they run trains by routes through the heart of the "railway desert" suggests that they have not been.

23. Short railway bridges are not difficult of repair. SHAEF was in error in estimating that the railway bridge over the canal between the Rivers Loire and Cher at Tours would require 20 days to be repaired for single-track working and 40 days for double-track. Single track through running was restored in about a week, after the attack of 23/5, if I remember correctly, and three tracks were open shortly thereafter. This bridge was 100′ in length. It follows that short bridges are not only hard to hit, because of their size, but are also easy to repair (in relative terms).

24. The discovery that a line has been salvaged for rail has led us to put it out of our minds. In the short run, this is entirely appropriate. It should be remembered, however, that a 10 mile stretch of line such as that between Chateaudun and Courtalain, can be very easily relaid by the Germans, particularly if by our failure to attack

it, we have put them on notice that we know it to be impassable. The road bed is intact. Bridges and engineering structures may be expected to be in good condition. And track laying, with rails from other portions of track effectively blocked which will not be used, should go far faster than the normal rate of a mile a day over country where a roadbed must be constructed. These stretches of track merit an occasional low-level oblique cover to determine whether rail is or is not laid.

Conclusions

25. These rather inchoate remarks may perhaps be drawn together in a series of summary statements:

    a) the enemy has been slow to move reserves to the Neptune; this hesitancy about sending them off has been largely due to fears of other landings. In these fears, the line of road and rail interdiction across the Seine has played a part.

    b) 21 Army Group has known with some degree of assurance the time of departure of German divisions from their bivouac areas; interruption of movement has been hindered by weather. It has on the other hand been aided by wide ranging fighters, including those of the 8th Air Force on other (escort) duties.

    c) the enemy was early enabled to detrain close to the battle area, by reason of the failure to cut Loire bridges before D-Day, and to block the Brittany peninsula. Thereafter general damage, extensive but ephemeral, has pushed him back from certain areas. Bridge blocks of long duration have pushed back detraining stations on other lines. The slowness of movement of 3 of the 4 panzer divisions south of the Loire made the penalty for delaying cutting the Loire bridges a light one.

    d) the enemy has been resourceful in
       i) ferrying the Seine
       ii) repairing superficial damage
       iii) circumventing incomplete blockages with the use of secondary lines
       iv) possibly using narrow gauge lines
       v) operating a railway system cut off from his main reserves of locomotives, rolling stock, coal, etc.

    e) the enemy has failed miserably to compensate for the loss of his bridges by either repair or new construction.

f) our performance, though hindered by weather, has been on the whole of outstanding efficiency. There is perhaps a tendency to lock the door after the horse is stolen, and a certain lacunae of information on line blocks, due to inadequate cover. Moreover certain leaks—Mezidon is outstanding—have taken a long time to plug. Nonetheless, the Air Forces, and the ground forces liasing with them, have some reason to be pleased so long as they are not blind to the several gaps in their treatment of the problem.

C. P. Kindleberger
Captain, AUS

Notes

1. The major accounts of this meeting, its antecedents, and subsequent developments related to it are to be found in Wesley Frank Craven and James Lea Cate (eds.), *The Army Air Forces in World War II*, vol. 3 (Chicago: University of Chicago Press, 1951), pp. 67–79, 138–166, 172–181. Sir Charles Webster and Noble Frankland, *The Strategic Air Offensive against Germany, 1939–1945*, vol. III (London: Her Majesty's Stationery Office, 1961); the whole of vol. III is relevant, but see especially pp. 10–41. Arthur William Tedder, *With Prejudice* (London: Cassell, 1966), pp. 499– 600, especially pp. 516–547. Solly Zuckerman, *From Apes to Warlords* (London: Hamish Hamilton, 1978), especially pp. 216–245; see the review of Zuckerman's book by C. P. Kindleberger in *Encounter* 51, no. 5 (November 1978): 39–42, Zuckerman's reply with Kindleberger's response, 52, no. 6 (June 1979): 86–89, and a further exchange between Zuckerman and the author in 55, nos. 2–3 (August– September 1980): 100–102.

    Other, less complete accounts are to be found in Gordon A. Harrison, *Cross-Channel Attack* (Washington, D.C.: GPO, 1951), pp. 217–230; Forrest C. Pogue, *The Supreme Command* (Washington, D.C.: GPO, 1954), pp. 123–134; Stephen E. Ambrose, *The Supreme Commander* (Garden City, N.Y.: Doubleday, 1969), pp. 363–376; Alfred P. Chandler et al. (eds.), *The Papers of Dwight David Eisenhower, The War Years: III* (Baltimore: Johns Hopkins University Press, 1970), pp. 1784–1787, for March 25 meeting; Haywood S. Hansell, Jr., *The Air Plan That Defeated Hitler* (Atlanta: Higgens-McArthur/Longino and Porter, 1972), especially pp. 186–192, 216–250, 267–278. Also Alfred Goldberg, "General Carl A. Spaatz," in *The War Lords*, ed. Field Marshal Sir Michael Carver (London: Weidenfeld and Weidenfeld, 1976), pp. 568–581; and David MacIsaac, *Strategic Bombing in World War Two: The Story of the United States Strategic Bombing Survey* (New York and London: Garland, 1976), especially pp. 17–20, 35, 75–77, 158. MacIsaac's Select Bibliography of Manuscript and Published Works bearing on strategic bombing (pp. 217–226) is particularly valuable.

An account of this affair, written by me in the late winter and spring of 1945, is contained in an unpublished manuscript, "Economic Outpost with Economic Warfare Division," vol. 5, "War Diary of the OSS, London: The Enemy Objectives Unit (EOU) to April 30, 1945," pp. 68–103; hereafter referred to as "EOU War Diary." The manuscript is to be found in the National Archives in Washington.

2. Webster and Frankland, *Strategic Air Offensive against Germany*, IV, 167–170.
3. Zuckerman, *From Apes to Warlords*, pp. 197–198.
4. Solly Zuckerman, "Bombs and Illusions in World War II," *Encounter* 52, no. 6 (June 1979): 86.
5. Zuckerman, *From Apes to Warlords*, p. 407 (Sicily Report, General Conclusions, paragraphs 10, 12, 14). Zuckerman here makes clearly the distinction between "tactical" and "strategical" targets he strongly denies making in *Encounter*, June 1979, p. 86. For some reason Zuckerman does not include in this appendix to *From Apes to Warlords* the nine brief paragraphs of Special Conclusions, which include his critically important negative assessment of bridges as "uneconomical and difficult targets."
6. Ibid., p. 239. There is an ambiguity here in Zuckerman's use of the phrase "factual analysis." Within the considerable limits of time for research and availability of evidence, well specified in the text of the Sicily Report, the facts in the text are no doubt correct. The analysis and conclusions drawn from them were, however, contestable, as is often the case, for the same set of facts can lend themselves to diverse interpretations. For example, the data presented in the text of the Sicily

Report on bridge attacks (pp. 56–60) lend themselves, as noted on pp. 39–40 and in note 41, to much more optimistic conclusions than were drawn from them by Tedder and Zuckerman.
7. Ibid., p. 217.
8. This is the date of the paper in the EOU files. Zuckerman dates the consideration of the AEAF/SHAEF plan as presented on February 15 (*Encounter*, June 1979, p. 86). In *From Apes to Warlords*, p. 222, a process is suggested in which there may have been a succession of amended drafts. It should, perhaps, be noted that while the plan promised to "paralyze movement in the whole region" the expected results in executing the plan as stated on March 25 by Tedder, Eisenhower, and Portal were more modest.
9. For a brief account of Tedder's RAF experience, see his *With Prejudice*, pp. 3–16.
10. A direct, personal account of the evolution of this plan is to be found in Hansell, *Air Plan That Defeated Hitler*, pp. 61–99. The official account is in Craven and Cate, *Army Air Forces*, I, 145–150.
11. A product of Wellington and Sandhurst, Hughes fought in the First World War and then served in the British army on the Indian northwest frontier, commanding troops in combat in every year down to 1929. In 1926, while on a boat to the United States, on leave, he met, and three months later married, an American girl, Frances Robertson Chase. In 1929 he retired from the Indian army and moved to St. Louis where, after initial vicissitudes, he managed a dairy farm with considerable success. In 1941 he was asked by a St. Louis friend, Malcolm Moss, an Army Air Corps reserve officer, and Haywood Hansell, a permanent Air Corps officer, to join the newly formed Air Plans Division of the Air Corps. He arrived in Washington in June 1941 and was promptly plunged into target selection for Germany and Japan. Moss and Hughes chose the target systems which were the basis for the calculations of the required number of sorties, attrition rates, production, training, etc. which entered into AWPD-1. He then made the transition to the staff of the incipient Eighth Air Force. He formed close and abiding ties to Spaatz and Fred L.

Anderson. Anderson became chief of Eighth Air Force Bomber Command under Ira Eaker and, in January 1944, Spaatz' deputy as commander of USSTAF. Hughes was a memorable figure in London: generally dealing with British and American commanders of much higher rank, his Air Force uniform bedecked with British army decorations of considerable distinction; his pockets bulging with highly classified papers; articulating his views with a gift for terse prose, selective profanity, and a stutter which often enhanced the effectiveness of his exposition. The war had a personal edge for him. Writing as of 1941 he says in his family memoir: "I did not love the Germans, who had quite recently killed my brother." His brother was the commander of the British aircraft carrier *Glorious*, lost off Norway in 1940.

12. Here, from his family memoir, is Hughes' account of his predicament and its resolution:

> One of my most pressing, immediate needs was for competent, capable people to examine, and evaluate for me, the mass of economic intelligence information being produced by the British Ministry of Economic Warfare. Such individuals just did not exist in the 8th Air Force, so I turned to the only other source of American personnel in England, the American Embassy in London. Our Ambassador was Mr. Winant, who had also been an American flier in World War I, and he had instructed the embassy officials to give our 8th Air Force every possible assistance. They had a small civilian economic section, and these people at once volunteered to do everything they could to help me. However, we all realized that this was not going to be nearly sufficient for my needs, so the Embassy cabled back to Washington describing the predicament which I was in, and requested that additional suitable personnel immediately be sent to assist in the task.
>
> This request caused a minor storm. Somehow the War Department heard of the cable, and General Marshall cabled to General Eisenhower, who had just taken over command of the European Theater, asking whether the

American Embassy in London was going to be permitted to direct the bombing operations of the 8th Air Force. General Eisenhower immediately called up General Spaatz, who sent for me, and the two of us next morning were ushered into General Eisenhower's office very much on the carpet. I explained to General Eisenhower the background of the whole episode. He immediately agreed with our urgent need for such assistance, and sent me to his Chief of Staff's office to, myself, draft out the answering cable to General Marshall. The storm subsided, and a few days later the first of the economists arrived by plane from America.

In fact, it took some negotiation and a bit more time to bring EOU to life. The OSS negotiations were conducted with Hughes by Edward Mason and Emile Despres; and the facts of life in the Washington bureaucracy decreed that the Board of Economic Warfare participate in the enterprise, an arrangement which brought John De Wilde and Nat Pincus into EOU and which otherwise worked well and comfortably.

13. The following chronology, drawn from my 1945 history of EOU, provides a summary portrait of who the members of EOU were and what they did:

13 September–mid-November 1942
Chandler Morse and Walt W. Rostow joined soon by John De Wilde, Harold J. Barnett, and William Salant started the unit, established contacts, studied intelligence sources; the materials and form of the Aiming Point reports were developed, culminating in the presentation and acceptance of the first finished reports.

Mid-November 1942–January 1943
Aiming Point reports focused around more relevant target systems and first outlines of bombing policy theory, culminated in a memorandum to Richard D. Hughes for Fred Anderson. Rapid build-up of general knowledgeability in intelligence sources and material.

January–February 1943
Further Aiming Point reports outlined; bombing policy

theory developed and refined, culminating in draft of plan for Pointblank (attack on German Air Force and ball-bearings), in accordance with the outlines of the Casablanca directive. Morse, Marc Peter, and Seymour Janow set up damage assessment unit at Princes Risborough. Charles P. Kindleberger arrived to take over from Morse on 28 February 1943.

February–August 1943
Large scale production of Aiming Point reports and evaluations of target systems, culminating in issuance of a handbook of target information. Kindleberger and Edward A. Mayer moved into aircraft field for first time, Rostow into aero engines; Irwin N. Pincus took over from De Wilde, and became assistant chief. Controversy with Air Ministry over timing of move of Focke-Wulfe Bremen to eastern Europe, culminated in Rostow's assignment in August to aircraft production section of Air Ministry Intelligence.

August–December 1943
Mayer and Rostow continued on German Air Force offensive; Pincus on ball-bearings and tank engines; Barnett started on oil; first speculation on tactical target problems. Salant and Phillip Coombs went to the Fifteenth Air Force in the Mediterranean.

January–April 1944
Work on strategic targets continued, culminated in work on USSTAF plan of March, advocating attack on oil; tactical target doctrine developed with Barnett at G-2 SHAEF. Marshalling yard plan, opposed by EOU, accepted in March but fight continued. Mark Kahn took over oil. Carl Kaysen and Robert Roosa began work on tactical targets.

May–Mid-August 1944
"Operation Octopus"—Kindleberger at 21st Army Group; Barnett at SHAEF; Kaysen at AEAF; Roosa, Kahn, Pincus, and Rostow [at night] continued at 40 Berkeley Square, advocating interdiction program, which gradually made headway. Joint Oil Target Committee organized. Rostow

was involved in bombing program directed against flying bombs and rockets.

Mid-August 1944–April 1945
Kindleberger and Roosa went with 12th Army Group. EOU continued with Pincus as chief, Kahn on oil target working committee, Kaysen and Barnett on transport and tanks, James Tyson on aircraft. Joint Oil Target Committee became the Combined Strategic Targets Committee, on which Pincus was EOU representative. Rostow continued at Air Ministry on aircraft (dispersal, underground factories, and jets).

14. "EOU War Diary," p. 17.
15. Adolf Galland, *The First and the Last* (New York: Holt, 1954; Bantam Edition, 1978), pp. 208–210 (Bantam ed.).
16. In a comment of April 8, 1980, on an earlier draft of this essay, General Andrew Goodpaster contributed the following observation on the efficacy of rail-line cuts:

> Incidentally, my own experience in Italy has some bearing on this. As the Germans retreated to Cassino they tore up the main line railroad for about 10 miles from Monte Lungo to Cassino, ripping the ties, twisting the rails and blowing up all of the many bridges and culverts. I had the task of converting the roadway into a road for tanks, and one of the most difficult parts of my task was to get access to the route at multiple points with heavy equipment and heavy material, rather than tackle it in linear fashion. I have some respect for multiple linear interdictionists.

17. The three-ring bridge interdiction plan, later incorporated in what was called the "Interdiction Handbook," was also called the Ballantine system in deference to a well-known beer advertisement of the time. It was later carried from EOU to G-2 SHAEF by Robert Roosa with strong support and subsequent advocacy of a British and an American major: Henry Bailey-King and George Rothman. For further references in the text, see pp. 72–74.
18. The following passage, in a letter from Eisenhower to Chur-

chill of May 2, 1944, suggests that the former was, indeed, fully aware of alternative proposals. But the evidence is that this letter (Chandler et al., *Eisenhower Papers, III*, p. 1843) was drafted by Tedder (see *With Prejudice*, pp. 528–529):

> I fear that there is still considerable misunderstanding regarding the nature of the object of my operations against enemy Rail transportation. It has never been suggested that these Operations by themselves will stop essential military movement. The object of the whole Operation is so to weaken and disorganize the Railway system as a whole that, at the critical time of the assault, German rail movements can be effectively delayed, and the rapid concentration of their forces against the lodgment area prevented. Time is the vital factor during the period immediately following the assault. The delay which would be involved by enforced use of Motor Transport in place of Railway Transport would, in itself, be of inestimable value.
>
> As regards alternative plans, at my Meeting with C.A.S. at which all authoritative military and expert opinion was represented, it was clear both to me and to the C.A.S., that there is no effective alternative plan. I have earnestly searched for these in my anxiety to avoid risking French antagonism toward the UK-US forces and governments. The alternatives suggested by U.S. Strategic Air Force and the Directorate of Bomber Operations, Air Ministry, have been fully and sympathetically considered. The suggestions subsequently made by the J.I.C. have also been studied. Some of these fit into the Tactical phase, and were already scheduled to be included in the final stage of the Air operations. They do not, themselves, however, in any way constitute a plan by which our Air power can, in the final stages, effectively delay and disrupt enemy concentrations.

19. Tedder, *With Prejudice*, p. 508.
20. Ibid., p. 513.
21. Ibid., p. 506.

22. Chandler et al., *Eisenhower Papers, III*, pp. 1784–1785.
23. Tedder, *With Prejudice*, p. 526.
24. As a working-level officer in the Air Ministry in 1943–1945, I was twice made aware of the extent of Churchill's involvement in detail. On one occasion a paper I had drafted on aircraft production arrived back on my desk, shortly after it was officially circulated, with a marginal notation about as follows in Churchill's hand: "ACAS/I [Assistant Chief of Air Staff, Intelligence] Pray sir, what is the basis for this extraordinary statement? W.C." The second occasion was more formidable. There was a major difference between two sections of air intelligence on the likely number of German daylight air sorties to be flown against the invading forces on D-Day. Those charged with studying the German order of battle estimated 2,000. Those who worked on German aircraft production and targeting estimated 200. Using Lord Cherwell in typical style, Churchill ordered an inquest climaxed by a formal debate in which I presented the case for the lower figure; a British colleague, Ronald Horne, for the higher. It was an interesting exercise marked by a contrast in styles. I presented in academic style the evidence we had, including its inadequacies and gaps, concluding why, on balance, I believed the lower figure more probable. Horne, a distinguished barrister, presented a straightforward advocate's case. Horne won. Cherwell and Churchill opted for the higher estimate; and a substantial fleet of U.S. fighter aircraft was assigned at Churchill's insistence to defensive operations on D-Day. Just how many German aircraft actually flew effective sorties against the landing forces on D-Day is not agreed in the official histories, depending, in part, on definitions used. Craven and Cate (*Army Air Forces*, III, 166) state: "Indeed, one of the most remarkable facts of the entire war is that the Luftwaffe did not make a single daylight attack on D-Day against Allied forces in the Channel or on the beaches." Using German sources, Harrison (*Cross-Channel Attack*, p. 335) estimates some 500 sorties, of which half were flown against shipping and a good many others were "chance encounters." By and large, both Horne and I grossly overestimated the effective strength

of the Luftwaffe on D-Day. For the vicissitudes of the German air force on D-Day, see Galland, *The First and the Last*, pp. 284–302 (chap. 32, "Where Is the Luftwaffe?").

25. Tedder (*With Prejudice*, pp. 516–517) had assessed the oil plan in these terms:

> I am frankly sceptical of the oil plan, partly because we have been led up that garden path before, partly because the targets are in difficult areas (six of them in the Ruhr, where we have been assured that the Americans could not do precision bombing on railway targets because of flak and smoke, and the most important ones in the areas south and southwest of Berlin, where penetration is most difficult), and partly because I am not sure as to the real vulnerability of the new synthetic oil plants, where the enemy has presumably taken immense precautions against an air attack by means of dispersal, protection, etc. I am even less impressed by the arguments advanced for the tank targets as a help for "Overlord."

26. Craven and Cate, *Army Air Forces*, III, 174. See also Webster and Frankland, *Strategic Air Offensive against Germany*, III, 46–47.
27. Craven and Cate, *Army Air Forces*, III, 174–176.
28. The incident is referred to by Hansell (*Air Plan That Defeated Hitler*, pp. 235–236). It was probably the background for the "verbal permission" Eisenhower granted Spaatz on April 19 to use the "next two good weather days" to attack oil installations in Germany (see pp. 55–56). Goldberg ("General Carl A. Spaatz," p. 574) also refers to Spaatz' resignation threat. In a conversation, Noble Frankland informed me that Spaatz confirmed this incident in an interview with Frankland.
29. Quoted in "EOU War Diary," p. 101.
30. Craven and Cate, *Army Air Forces*, III, 372–378. Some odd things went on in the Mediterranean toward the end of 1943. In the brief interval between Spaatz' departure for London and Eaker's arrival, a virtual embargo on bridge attacks was ordered by Tedder's headquarters on December 24, 1943, and seven northern Italian marshalling yards were accorded overriding priority among transport targets. On that day the

Target Section of MAAF recommended "complete, simultaneous, and continuous cutting of all German supply lines" across central Italy. It took several months to resolve this confusion. Sir John Slessor, who left Coastal Command to become Eaker's deputy in the Mediterranean, played an important part in settling the conceptual battle over transport targets left in the wake of Tedder's and Zuckerman's departure for Britain. Here is Slessor's account of why he disengaged from Tedder's doctrine and helped lay the basis for Operation STRANGLE (*The Central Blue* [London: Cassell, 1956], p. 568):

> ... there was at least one conclusion in the report [Zuckerman's Sicily Report] which had since been invalidated by experience, namely that bridges as targets were too uneconomical and difficult to be worth attacking except in special circumstances in the tactical area.
>
> In general I felt that this controversy was somewhat unreal. The fact that a certain technique had undoubtedly been successful in one set of circumstances did not necessarily mean it would always be so—and anyway there seemed no reason why it should be adopted to the exclusion of all others. It depended on a number of things—such as the time factor, how quickly one wanted results, and on the forces available. The thing to do was to adapt one's thinking to the conditions at the time and to the developing capacity of aircraft and weapons, making full use of the flexibility of air-power to attack the enemy transportation system in the way that seemed most likely to be profitable in the conditions with which we were faced, and with the resources we had at our disposal.
>
> Moreover, looking at the map of Italy with its relatively few railways, it seemed from the lessons of the past at least possible that we had here a special opportunity for really decisive results. In a memorandum dated February 11 to the very able young Director of Operations, Brigadier-General Lauris Norstad, calling for a review of bombing policy, I wrote—
>
> "There are now some seventeen German divisions in

Italy south of Rome. I do not believe the Army—even with our support—will move them. But I think it more than possible that the Hun, by concentrating all this force so far south, has given us—the Air Forces—an opportunity. He has been able up to now just to support his smaller armies on the present line in spite of our air attacks on his communications. I find it hard to believe that, by increasing those forces, he has not put a load on to his communications which they will not be able to stand if we really sustain a scientifically planned offensive *against the right places* in his L. of C."

Subsequent discussions led to the production of a new bombing directive, which was approved by Eaker and issued on February 18.

31. Ibid., pp. 157–162.
32. Harrison, *Cross-Channel Attack*, p. 228. William F. Whitmore concludes as follows ("Logistics as a Target System," *Journal of Defense Research* 2B, no. 2 [Summer 1970]: 188): "World War II experience, both in Italy and in Normandy, indicated that fighter/bombers (dive and glide bombing) could cut bridges for 50 to 60 tons a cut, medium bombers (level bombing from, say, 10,000 feet) for 100 to 120 tons, and 'heavies' (B-17 and RAF Bomber Command) for something over 200 tons. These were average figures for normal squadrons, and they were frequently improved on in particular cases. In the few instances where Air Force policy allowed squadrons to specialize in 'bridge-busting' (that is, the use of AZON guided bombs in Burma), spectacular results were obtained—as low as 4 or 5 tons per cut."
33. This historian's problem recalls a dictum of Arnold Toynbee (*A Study of History*, vol. X [Oxford: Oxford University Press, 1954], p. 227), quoted by MacIsaac, *Strategic Bombing in World War Two*, p. 217: "The information that is to be found in an official document will have been put there—if we may assume that the document has been drafted competently—in order to serve some official purpose which, whatever it may have been, will certainly not have been the irrelevant purpose of informing a future historian."

34. Charles P. Kindleberger, "World War II Strategy," *Encounter* 51, no. 5 (November 1978): 41.
35. As noted in the text, three other bridges were attacked on that day. It is possible that, in memory, General Smith confused the dramatic results of the destruction of the nearby explosives factory with mining of the Vernon bridge. As the text notes, his memory of the number of sorties required per bridge as then estimated by opponents of bridge attacks, is almost certainly too low.
36. Tedder, *With Prejudice*, p. 537. Tedder does not, however, provide an account of how the attacks on bridges were introduced. He dates the major attacks on bridges as beginning as late as May 21. Zuckerman continues to fight the bridges to the end in his book (*From Apes to Warlords*, pp. 282–283); but he shifts ground somewhat in his reply to Kindleberger (*Encounter*, June 1979, pp. 86–89). He argues, in effect, that bridges were always part of the transport plan but that their attack was not as effective as the assault on marshalling yards.
37. Craven and Cate, *Army Air Forces* (III, 689–711), contains a full and vivid account of air operations in response to the German offensive. The plan applied to inhibit the bringing forward of German men and supplies during the Battle of the Bulge was a quick adaptation of one designed to support an Allied offensive which was pre-empted by the German attack. In its details the plan was worked out by Kindleberger and Roosa, both by this time thoroughly experienced practitioners of the art of target selection for purposes of tactical interdiction. The successful use of air power during the Battle of the Bulge, after the weather cleared, laid the conceptual groundwork for the Ruhr interdiction scheme. Hughes, at the time Vandenberg's target planner at the Ninth Air Force headquarters, played an important role in designing and, especially, gaining acceptance for the target plan that went into effect when the weather broke favorable. In his family memoir Hughes describes the subsequent origins of the Ruhr interdiction scheme in a style rather different from the official military histories (pp. 62–64):

> With the continued success of both our ground armies

and our air forces, all the desperate heartbreaking decisions of the past were over, and such problems as arose were relatively minor.

One of these was caused by, of all things, *Time Magazine*. The mail from America brought the latest copy of *Time*, with General Vandenberg's picture on the front cover. Inside was a long article, mainly complimentary to him and his Ninth Air Force. However, one paragraph made the General almost frantic. Largely by inference, it accused him of being too closely tied to the wishes of the ground force Generals, and possibly lacking in the breadth of strategic thought so desirable in an Air Force Commander, as compared to the thinking of the pedestrian slow-moving ground soldiers! There was no validity in this implied criticism whatsoever, but the printed, published, word scared the insecure Vandenberg almost to death. His reaction was violent. It assumed two aspects. First, who could have inspired the paragraph, General Spaatz, General Arnold, or who? Secondly, what could he do quickly to disprove the accusation? I was sent for in a hurry, the situation rapidly explained to me, and an appeal made to me to dream up some semi-strategic operation immediately.

I went back to my office, inwardly laughing, and considered the various possibilities. The problem, of course, was to assuage the General's vanity, yet to do so without getting anybody hurt. A possible answer, with the necessary glamorous over-tones, quickly became apparent. "Interdict the Ruhr by tactical air power."

It was obvious that our ground forces were about to surround and cut off the Ruhr in short order, but just enough time probably remained for General Vandenberg to make a grandstand play. I instructed the target section to prepare the usual war room map portraying the railroad and highway bridges, which, if destroyed, would prevent movement in and out of the Ruhr, and took the job, all prettied-up in various colors, to General Vandenberg. He pounced on it like a starving lion, and immediately ordered his personal pilot to fly us down to Paris to

General Eisenhower's headquarters. On arrival there, we proudly displayed the plan to the SHAEF air planners, and obtained their consent to put it into immediate execution. Public relations officers were called in from all sides and semi-confidentially briefed on the 9th Air Force intentions.

We flew back and I sent out the necessary target priorities to 9th Air Force Bomber Command and to the three Tactical Air Commands. The targets involved were no more difficult, or hazardous, than those which they were attacking every day in the course of normal operations, so my conscience remained fairly clear.

As we destroyed the last selected target, the ground forces completed their encirclement, but in General Vandenberg's mind his professional reputation was saved.

38. Craven and Cate (*Army Air Forces*, III, 160–162) capture well the dispassionate historian's dilemma in the face of the mixed evidence:

> Whether the rail center attacks—subject of a long controversy among invasion planners in early 1944—had been necessary or not in accomplishing the wreckage of Germany's transportation system continued to be a subject of some debate. Even the German commanders held varying opinions, and captured enemy records can be interpreted to support several points of view. Von Rundstedt later told interrogators that strategic bombing had little or no effect on the French railway systems until late in July 1944. The German officer who was in charge of military transport on railways in the west stressed the catastrophic effects of Allied interdiction, especially bridge-breaking. Other enemy evidence indicated that the attritional bombings of the railway repair centers and marshalling yards were decisive in stopping traffic. The fact remained that the Germans suffered indescribable and often ludicrous difficulties in moving their troops and supplies, whether in reinforcement or evacuation.
>
> Allied opinion about the different aspects of the transportation campaign remained consistent; those who had

sponsored the rail center bombings in the first place generally thought they had been right, and the champions of interdiction continued to argue their side of the case. The evidence, Germany's ruined communications, lent itself to a variety of interpretation. In November 1944, shortly before he lost his life on a flight to India, Leigh-Mallory presented to Eisenhower a "despatch" summarizing the AEAF's contributions. It is not surprising that he hailed the rail center program as fully realized and claimed that his beliefs had been confirmed. Solly Zuckerman prepared two studies after the invasion in which statistics seemed to prove the higher importance of attrition as compared to interdiction. General Brereton and Air Marshal Harris, both of whom had favored the rail center campaign, looked back upon it after the war as very effective in bringing about the results they had intended. Air Marshal Tedder said the rail center bombings had been the main factor in producing the collapse of German communications, an achievement which he said had come about more rapidly and more completely than he had anticipated. SHAEF G-2 reversed its position of May 1944 to conclude in November that attrition had proved more effective in France before D-Day than interdiction. And there was scattered support from other analyses to justify the rail center bombings. Perhaps most telling of all was the decision of the Allies to continue bombing rail centers, which they did until the end of the war, though not without differences over the probable effectiveness of such attacks and doubts about results.

On the other hand, SHAEF G-2 in May and June 1944 assessed the attrition campaign as a severe disappointment, if not an alarming failure. As late as D plus 1 the Germans seemed to possess several times the railway resources they needed, a fact which, if true, refuted the champions of attrition. Two Ninth Air Force studies of July 1944 judged the attrition program as having almost no effect in isolating Normandy, while interdiction was considered decisive. General Spaatz and most USSTAF officers continued to look upon the rail center bombings as much less important than bridge-breaking and line-cutting, and General Arnold seems to have agreed. The U.S. Embassy's railway experts likewise remained consistent by deciding a few months after OVERLORD that interdiction had been the decisive phase of the transportation campaign. A comprehensive study of the U.S. Strategic Bombing Survey compiled under the direction of Gen. Omar N. Bradley soon after V-E Day drew a similar conclusion. Also, the president of the French railway system said rail attacks were less significant than those on bridges. Finally, an AAF evaluation board report based largely on French railway records concluded after a laborious examination of evidence and balancing of factors: "The pre–D-day attacks against French rail centers were not necessary, and the 70,000 tons involved could have been devoted to alternative targets."

39. Whitmore's essay ("Logistics as a Target System") was prepared in the autumn of 1952, against the background of his earlier work, to illuminate tactical bombing problems during the Korean War.
40. Ibid., pp. 189–190. Both Tedder and Zuckerman include in their memoirs charts exhibiting the decline in French rail traffic after transport bombing began (*With Prejudice*, opposite p. 541, down to May 28, 1944; *From Apes to Warlords*, p. 299, down to the end of July). They exhibit a radical decline in total traffic, much more modest declines in military traffic. The broad picture that emerges is consistent with Whitmore's appraisal and the argument of the interdictionists, as Kindleberger notes (*Encounter*, November 1978, p. 41). The charts recall Churchill's anxiety, expressed to Eisenhower in a letter of April 29, 1944, that 90 percent of the French railway system would have to be knocked out before any valuable military effects began to occur (Webster and Frankland, *Strategic Air Offensive against Germany*, III, 37).
41. Kindleberger, *Encounter*, November 1978, p. 41.
42. In the course of writing this book I subjected the data in the text of Zuckerman's Sicily Report to regression analysis to establish the requirements they implied for an 80 percent

probability under each of the three categories using a conservative hyperbolic exponential equation, in which one approaches but never reaches 100 percent. The results, as they flowed from the computer, were these:

	Tonnage	
	Rail	Road
80% hit	396.51	300.17
80% blocked	409.11	319.25
80% traffic impeded	125.45	308.49

The average tonnage actually required to block the Seine bridges before D-Day proved to be about 220 per bridge (Harrison, *Cross-Channel Attack*, p. 228); that is, the 1944 Western European experience proved to be roughly consistent with 1943 experience in the Mediterranean. In our exchange on this matter in *Encounter* (August– September, 1980, pp. 100–102), Zuckerman, using a different statistical method, comes up with a not grossly dissimilar result. The point is that the data in the Sicily Report did not justify in any way the figure of 1,200 tons per bridge which became fixed in Tedder's and Leigh-Mallory's minds, although Zuckerman now takes his distance from that figure. I might take the occasion to say that I share the reserve expressed by Zuckerman in our 1980 exchange about excessive reliance on regression analysis. I simply wished to check by a more sophisticated method the conclusion at which EOU had arrived early in 1944 by simple arithmetic.

43. In the slightly longer run Whitmore ("Logistics as a Target System," p. 183) concludes that a considerable cost was paid by the Allies for the marshalling-yard attacks:

> . . . the rail center attacks did render the rail system largely useless to the Allies in breaking out of the invasion area. The Germans could avoid the use of marshalling yards by making up their military trains in Germany and running them straight through. Line cuts in the centers could be avoided by switching. The Allies found themselves unable to assemble trains in the bombed area, and resorted to high-speed truck convoys, the so-called "Red Ball Highway." These were less efficient load carriers than

freight cars, and the high speeds over poor roads produced rapid attrition of the available trucks. The cost of this operation seems properly chargeable to the rail center attacks.

44. Webster and Frankland (*Strategic Air Offensive against Germany*, III, 225–227) note that the oil experts overestimated German production, consumption, and stocks, but these errors, in part compensating, did not prevent changes in the oil situation from being quite accurately estimated.
45. Charles Curtis, *A Commonplace Book* (New York: Simon and Schuster, 1957), pp. 112–113.
46. Albert Speer, *Inside the Third Reich* (New York: Macmillan, 1970), p. 346.
47. Quoted in Webster and Frankland, *Strategic Air Offensive against Germany*, III, 239–240; see, also, five of Speer's reports to Hitler on the effects of the attacks on oil, ibid., IV, 321–340. For a recent brief review of the oil offensive, with special emphasis on its consequences for oil storage facilities and stocks, see Edmund Dews, *POL Storage as a Target for Air Attack: Evidence from the World War II Allied Air Campaigns against Enemy Oil Installations* (Santa Monica, Calif.: RAND, June 1980; a RAND Note, N-1523-PA&E).
48. Galland, *The First and the Last*, pp. 224–226.
49. Sir Arthur Harris, *Bomber Offensive* (London: Collins, 1947), p. 220.
50. Webster and Frankland, *Strategic Air Offensive against Germany*, III, 242–243.
51. Slessor, *The Central Blue*, p. 521.
52. Dwight D. Eisenhower, *Crusade in Europe* (Garden City, N.Y.: Doubleday, 1948), pp. 74–75.
53. F. M. Sallagar, *Operation "STRANGLE" (Italy, Spring 1944): A Case Study of Tactical Air Interdiction* (Santa Monica, Calif.: RAND, R-851-PR, February 1972).
54. Ibid., pp. 60–79. Sallagar's net assessment, while a careful and independent piece of research based on multiple sources, conforms substantially to Slessor's (*The Central Blue*, especially pp. 566–585). Slessor's fundamental assessment, which holds up well, was set down in memoranda to Portal of April and June 1944.

Index

AAF Evaluation Board, 73, 155 n
Acheres, 126, 130
Achiet-le-Grande, 126
AEAF (Allied Expeditionary Air Force), 3, 46, 66; bombing plan of, 14, 36, 38–39, 42, 141 n; and bridge attacks, 56; contributions of, 154 n
Africa, 20, 91
Aircraft: fighter bombers (P-47), 28, 59, 61, 63–64, 114, 117–118, 150 n; heavy bombers (B-17 and B-24), 10, 31, 46, 48, 53–54, 66–67, 76, 95, 113, 150 n; jet fighters (Me. 262), 120; long-range fighters (P-51), 25, 27–28, 64; medium bombers (B-26), 59, 64, 150 n; night fighters (German), 19; single-engine fighters (German), 25–26, 28; Typhoon (British single-engine fighter-bomber), 59
Aircraft industry: attacks on, 24, 26–27, 31; production, 53, 108–109
Air Ministry, British, 16, 39, 50, 69, 110, 116, 119, 146 n
Air Staff, British, 3, 18, 22. *See also* Portal, Charles
Air supremacy, 5–6, 16, 28, 37, 56, 85, 92

Albert Canal, 59, 126
Alderney, 8–9
Alençon, 126–127
Algiers, 9
Ambrose, Stephen E., 139 n
Amiens, 63, 124–126, 135
Ammunition dumps, 41–42, 47–48
Anderson, Frederick L., 3, 18, 22, 26, 45, 88, 141 n–142 n, 143 n; and bridge attacks, 58, 64; and oil attacks, 32, 34–35, 37, 76, 94
Anderson, Orvil, 45
Angoulême, 127, 130
Antwerp, 83, 135
Ardennes, 69, 81
Argentan, 125–127, 132, 134
Armaments production, 108–109
Arnold, Henry H. (Hap), 50, 53, 107, 109, 152 n, 155 n
Atlantic Wall, 60
Attrition, 69, 73–74, 153 n–154 n
Aulnoye, 135
Australia, 20
Avranches, 126, 135
AWPD-1 (Air War Plans Division—Plan 1), 16, 141 n

Bailey-King, Henry, 145 n
Balkans, 115
Ballantine system (three rings of bridges), 145 n

159

Ball bearing industry, 26–27, 31, 89, 94. *See also* POINTBLANK
Barnett, Harold H., 42, 112, 143 n, 145 n
Battle of Britain, 16, 25, 30
Battle of the Bulge, 67, 69, 119, 151 n
Bavarian Alps, 70
Bay of Biscay, 124
Beaugency, 131
Belgium, 36, 45, 51, 59, 73, 125
Berlin, 70, 111, 148 n
Bernay, 128
BEW (Board of Economic Warfare), 17, 143 n
Big Week, the (Feb. 20–25, 1944), 27, 31, 37–38, 80
Birmingham, 8
Blois, 60
Bombing: area, 4, 6, 8, 19, 22, 25, 70, 86, 96, 110–112; industrial, 18, 20, 99–104; pattern, 21; precision, 16, 19, 21–22, 25, 30, 96, 148 n
Bombs: AZON guided, 150 n; delayed fuse, 61
Bomb tonnage, 26, 60–61, 73, 75, 79, 103, 150 n, 156 n
Bonacourt, 132
Bordeaux, 125, 127
Bottomley, Norman, 88
Boulogne, 124
Bradley, Omar N., 119, 155 n
Brant, E. D., 59
Brereton, Lewis, 58–59, 154 n
Bridge attacks, 5, 72, 84, 86; advocates of, 41–42, 51, 58, 75; bomb tonnage for, 150 n; evaluations of, 153 n–155 n; events leading to, 56–65; in Mediterranean campaign, 39, 41, 57–58, 62, 116, 148 n–149 n; methods of, 61–63; time factor in, 48; at Vernon, 116–118; Zuckerman's views on, 11–12, 56, 140 n
Brittany, 125, 127, 133, 136

Bueil, 126
Bufton, Sidney, 18
Burma, 150 n

Cabell, Charles Pearré, 32, 45
Caen, 126
Cairo, 9, 15
Calais, 59
Call, Lance, 116–118
Carver, Michael, 140 n
CAS. *See* Portal, Charles
Casablanca directive, 11, 24, 144 n
Cassino, 145 n
Cate, James Lea, 53, 139 n, 141 n, 147 n–148 n, 151 n, 153 n
Chandler, Alfred P., 139 n, 146 n–147 n
Chartres, 124–127, 131
Chase, Frances Robertson (Mrs. Richard D'Oyly Hughes), 141 n
Chateaudun, 126–127, 135
Chemnitz, 70
Cherbourg, 8
Cherisy, 131, 134
Cher River, 135
Cherwell, Lord (Frederick Lindemann), 51, 147 n
Churchill, Winston, 77, 83, 147 n; and bridge attacks, 64–65; and Eisenhower, 51, 145 n–146 n, 155 n; and Leigh-Mallory, 46; and marshalling yard attacks, 5, 50–51, 155 n
Civilian casualties, 4, 42, 51, 98
CLARION, 70
Cloyes, 131
COA (Committee of Operations Analysts), 107
Coltainville, 131
Combat formations, 29
Command, problems of, 49–50, 77, 83–85
Communications, collapse of, 154 n
Compiegne, 135
Coombs, Phillip, 144 n

Counteroffensive. *See* Battle of the Bulge
Courtalain, 135
Courville, 126
Craven, Wesley Frank, 53, 139 n, 141 n, 147 n–148 n, 151 n, 153 n
Creil, 135
CROSSBOW, 48, 56
CSTC (Combined Strategic Target Committee), 66, 70, 145 n
Curtis, Charles, 77, 85, 157 n

D'Aurelio (Italian General), 57
Denmark, 124, 135
Despres, Emile, 143 n
DeWilde, John, 143 n
Dews, Edmund, 157 n
Dieppe, 106, 124
Diplomacy, postwar, 82–83
Dol, 125–126, 133
Domfront, 127
Douglass, Kingman, 119
Dresden, 70
Dreux, 126, 131–132
Duclair, 128

Eaker, Ira, 58, 142 n, 148 n, 150 n
Eighth Air Force, 21, 44, 70, 125, 136; and bridge attacks, 62, 130; capabilities of, 24, 32; and Hughes, 141 n–142 n; and marshalling yard attacks, 45, 96, 98, 131; and oil attacks, 56, 78, 80; and Spaatz, 114–115
Eisenhower, Dwight D., 3, 16, 32, 88, 95, 142 n–143 n, 145 n, 157 n; and AEAF, 43, 154 n; April 17 directive of, 5–6, 55; and Churchill, 51, 145 n–146 n, 155; on landing issues, 48–49; leadership of, 83–85; and marshalling yard attacks, 4–5, 14, 83–84, 93, 97, 141 n; and oil attacks, 54, 66, 77, 95, 98, 148 n; and Ruhr plan, 153 n; and Spaatz, 44–45, 48, 113–114; and Tedder, 46–47; on use of air power, 6, 50, 56, 91–92, 95–96
El Alamein, 9
EOU (Enemy Objectives Unit), 24, 31, 66, 87; and bridge attacks, 145 n; history of, 17–18, 142 n–143 n; and marshalling yard attacks, 15–16, 36–39, 41, 67, 69, 144 n; and oil attacks, 31–33, 76, 145 n; and target selection, 20–23, 36, 40–43, 99–112, 143 n–145 n, 156 n; war diary of, 140 n, 145 n, 148 n
Epernon, 131
Erquelines, 135
Etampes, 131
European Advisory Commission, 83
Evreaux, 126, 132
Ezra, Derek, 123

Falaise, 133
Fécamp, 117
Fifteenth Air Force, 26, 44, 115; capabilities of, 31–32; and marshalling yard attacks, 54, 96, 98; and oil attacks, 52–53, 55, 80
Flers, 126, 127
Focke-Wulf factory, Bremen, 144 n
Folligny, 127
Foret de Cinglais, 133
Foret d'Ecouves, 134
Foret de la Londe, 129
Forgan, 133
Fougeres, 127, 133
Fourteen Points, the, 112
France: advance of Allied armies through, 66; contribution of, to German war effort, 91, 111; food distribution in, 91; retreat of enemy across, 86; underground in, 72. *See also* Bridge attacks; Marshalling yard attacks; Movement, enemy

Frankland, Noble, 139 n–140 n, 148 n, 157 n
Fuel dumps, 41–43, 48

Galland, Adolf, 28–30, 78–79, 145 n, 148 n, 157 n
Ghent, 135
Goldberg, Alfred, 140 n, 148 n
Goodpaster, Andrew, 77, 145 n
Grande Ceinture, 126
Granville, 125
Ground forces, 87, 156 n

Hamburg, 19, 111
Hansell, Haywood, 139 n, 141 n, 148 n
Harris, Arthur, 3–6, 88, 157 n; and area bombing, 7, 19, 80, 84, 95–96; and marshalling yard attacks, 96, 154 n; military goals of, 46; and oil attacks, 80–82; status of, 48–50, 77
Harrison, Gordon A., 139 n, 147 n, 150 n, 156 n
Hitler, Adolph, 84, 110, 157 n
Honerkamp, Roselene, 17
Honfleur, 128
Horne, Ronald, 147 n
Hughes, Richard O'Oyly, 31, 36–37, 40, 44, 52, 119; background of, 16–17, 22, 141 n; and EOU, 17–19; and Ruhr plan, 151 n–153 n; and USSTAF plan, 32
Hull, 8

Inglis, Frank, 88
Intelligence, 21, 23, 52, 120, 125
Interdiction, 10, 18, 57–58, 70, 73–74, 86, 121, 151 n, 154 n
Interdiction Handbook, 145 n
Italy, 16, 40, 111, 150 n. *See also* Mediterranean campaign; Operation STRANGLE

Janow, Seymour, 144 n

Japan, 20, 73, 141 n
JIC (Joint Intelligence Committee), 50, 91, 95, 146 n
JIS (Joint Intelligence Staff), 3, 88
Jugon, 127
Juvisy, 126, 130–131

Kahn, Mark, 42, 144 n–145 n
Kaysen, Carl, 38, 42, 45, 66, 144 n
Kesselring, Albert, 57
Kindleberger, Charles P., 21, 119, 151 n, 155 n; and bridge attacks, 63; and target selection, 32, 36, 42, 143 n–145 n; on Zuckerman, 74, 139 n
Kingston-McCloughry, E. J., 13
Korean War, 155 n

La Brohiniere, 127
La Chappelle Athenaise, 127
La Fleche, 127
Laigle, 132
La Loupe, 126
Laval, 127
Lawrence, Oliver, 19, 34–35, 39, 66, 76, 89
Le Bourget, 135
Le Havre, 128
Leigh-Mallory, Trafford, 3, 61, 88–89; background of, 15; and bridge attacks, 56, 59–60, 62–64, 156 n; and marshalling yard attacks, 154 n; status of, 47, 49, 77; and target selection, 95, 97; and Zuckerman, 7, 13–14
Le Mans, 127
Lens, 90
Leuna, 61
L'Hermitage, 126
Lille, 90, 135
Lisieux, 128, 132
Loire River: bridge attacks on, 42, 48, 56, 59, 62–64, 73, 135–136; and enemy movement, 127, 129–130, 131, 134
Ludendorff, Erich, 112

Luftwaffe, 4, 37, 55, 78–79, 81, 147 n–148 n

MAAF (Mediterranean Allied Air Forces), 57, 149 n
MacIsaac, David, 140 n, 150 n
McMullen, General (War Office), 88, 90, 93
Mailly, 124
Maintenon, 126, 134
Mantes, 59, 126, 131, 134
Mantes Gassicourt, 126
Marshall, George, 5, 49, 142 n–143 n
March 25 meeting, 3–5, 49, 88–98, 139 n
March 25 decision: character of, 72; Churchill's delay of, 50; effects of, 78, 83. *See also* Marshalling yard attacks
Marshalling yard attacks: adoption of plan for, 5, 14, 70–72, 76; alternatives to, 5, 31–32, 43, 47, 93–95; bomb tonnage for, 79; and bridge attacks, 59; and Casablanca directive, 24; and Churchill, 50; debate over, 3–5, 12, 45, 50–51, 67, 69–71, 75–77, 88–98, 153 n–154 n; effects of, 37, 59–60, 76, 135–137, 141 n, 153 n–157 n; and Eisenhower, 93, 145 n–146 n; and enemy movement, 89–94, 122–137; evaluations of, 59, 78, 92, 131; in Mediterranean campaign, 4, 9, 12, 36, 38–41, 57, 75, 91–92, 148 n; modification of plan for, 64–65, 67, 69; and oil attacks, 32, 55, 76, 79; and planning paper of January 22, 1944, 14; and Rostow's December 12, 1944, memorandum, 119–121; Spaatz on, 44–45, 54, 93, 113–115; Tedder on, 3–4, 13, 46–47, 88–91; Zuckerman on, 9–11, 13–14, 36, 155 n

Masey Palaiseau, 126
Mason, Edward S., 19, 143 n
Massy, 130
MATAF (Mediterranean Allied Tactical Air Forces), 57
Matelots, 130
Mayenne, 127
Mayer, Edward A., 144 n
Mediterranean campaign, 26, 105, 148 n; bomb tonnage for, 156 n; influence of, 38, 45, 47, 56; and German morale, 110
Messina Straits, 39
Meulan, 126, 131
Meuse River, 56, 59, 62–63
MEW (Ministry of Economic Warfare), 18–19, 50, 69, 94, 142 n
Mezidon, 127, 132
Military Supplies Working Committee, 66–67, 69
Ministry of Home Security, 7
Miraumont, 126
Monancourt, 126
Mons, 135
Monte Lungo, 145 n
Montfort, 127
Montgomery, Bernard, 59, 83
Mont St. Michel, 127
Morale, German, 8, 110–112
Morley, Arthur, 18
Morse, Chandler, 17, 143 n
Mortague-au-Perche, 127
Moss, Malcolm, 141 n
Mountbatten, Louis, 8
Mouscron, 135
Movement, enemy, 58, 60, 73–74, 90–94, 122–137

Nantes, 125, 131
NEPTUNE, 63, 89, 124, 129, 136
Ninth Air Force, 59, 64, 95, 134, 151 n–154 n
Noble, Andrew, 89, 91
Normandy, 86, 121, 150 n; and air support, 59, 86; enemy movement near, 59, 60, 72; as landing site, 38, 44, 64, 73, 154 n

163

Norstad, Lauris, 149 n
Norway, 142 n

OBOE, 96
Oder River, 69
Oil attacks, 56, 66–67, 70, 78, 80, 119, 157 n; as alternative to marshalling yard attacks, 4, 5, 31, 34–35, 37, 43, 49, 52, 84; background of, 32, 55–56, 64–65, 148 n; and Casablanca directive, 24; Churchill on, 50; debate over, 46, 93–95, 148 n; delay of, 72, 76–78, 82; effects of, 4, 53–54, 76, 78–81, 86, 93–95; and EOU, 42, 144 n; in Germany, 52, 55, 61, 81, 113; in Romania, 52–55, 95, 113–114; Spaatz on, 4, 44, 54, 56, 93, 113–115
Oil stocks, estimates of, 33–34, 52–53, 76, 94, 157 n
Oissel, 59
OKW (Western High Command), 79
Operation STRANGLE, 39, 58–59, 65, 75, 86, 149 n
Orival, 59
Orleans, 127, 130–131
OSS (Office of Strategic Services), 17, 19–20, 57, 140 n, 143 n
OVERLORD, 13, 34, 88, 97, 148 n, 155 n; and air power, 30, 37, 42, 86, 91, 113–115; and Eisenhower's memorandum of March 22, 1944, 48–49; and marshalling yard attacks, 89, 93, 97; and oil attacks, 35, 54, 94–95; and Tedder, 46, 56

Palaiseau, 130
Pantelleria, 9–10
Panzer divisions, 73, 124–131, 135–136
Paris, 60, 73, 125, 127, 130–131, 152 n

Part, A. A., 122–123
Pas de Calais, 62, 72
Patton, George, 83
Persan Beaumont, 135
Peter, Marc, 144 n
Photography, use of, 125, 133–134
Pincus, Irwin N., 143 n–145 n
Ploeşti, 52–55, 113–114
Pogue, Forrest C., 139 n
POINTBLANK, 24, 32, 48–49, 55, 144 n. *See also* Ball bearing industry
Poissy, 126, 131
Poitiers, 124–125, 130
Pontaubault, 126, 134
Pontoson, 126
Portal, Charles, 3, 24, 27, 43, 46, 88, 115, 157 n; command problems of, 49–50, 77; and March 25 meeting, 89–90, 94–95, 97–98; and marshalling yard attacks, 4, 97, 141 n; and oil attacks, 32, 35, 76, 80–82
Port Boulet, 127, 129
Po Valley, 58

Quillebeuf, 128

Radar, use of, 25, 130
RAF Bomber Command, 3, 44–45, 114; and area bombing, 4, 19, 24–25, 70, 96; capabilities of, 6, 14, 18; and EOU, 21; and marshalling yard attacks, 96, 126, 130–131; and oil attacks, 65–66, 80
Reconnaissance, 133–135
"Red Ball Highway," 157 n
Redon, 125, 134
Rennes, 125–127, 133–134
Rhine River, 70
Richardson (British Brigadier General), 63
Rommel, Erwin, 9
Roosa, Robert, 41–42, 122, 144 n–145 n, 151 n

Roosevelt, Franklin, 5, 51, 83
Romania, 52–54, 95, 115. *See also* Ploeşti
Rostow, Walt W., 21, 32, 52, 63, 76, 147 n, 155 n–156 n; and EOU, 17, 140 n, 143 n–145 n; memorandum of, on bombing policy, 119–121; memorandum of, on German morale, 110–112
Rothman, George, 145 n
Rouen, 128
Ruhr, 19, 69, 80, 148 n, 151 n–152 n
Rundstedt, Karl Rudolf Gerd von, 60, 67, 119, 153 n
Russia, 20, 69, 81–82, 110

Sable-sur-Sarthe, 127
St. Gauberge, 128
St. Hilaire, 127, 134
St. Lo, 73
St. Medard-sur-Ille, 133
Salant, William, 99–104, 143 n–144 n
Sallager, F. M., 86, 157 n
Schlatter, David, 64
Second Tactical Air Force, British, 62–63, 95, 153 n
Seine River: attacks on bridges, 5, 42, 56, 59–60, 62–63, 73, 130, 156 n; and enemy movement, 125, 128–129, 131, 136
SHAEF (Supreme Headquarters Allied Expeditionary Force), 3, 36, 67, 122, 135, 153 n, 154 n; and bridge attacks, 59, 73, 135, 145 n; and marshalling yard attacks, 69–70, 124
Sicily, 10–13, 36, 38–39, 75. *See also* Mediterranean campaign
Sicily Report, 12, 75, 140 n, 149 n, 155 n–156 n
Sille le Guillaume, 127
Slessor, John, 84, 149 n, 157 n
Smith, Frederic H., 63, 151 n
Smuts, Jan Christiaan, 84

Sotteville, 128–129
Spaatz, Carl, 3–4, 18, 27, 35, 77, 88, 148 n, 152 n; and bridge attacks, 58–59, 62, 65, 154 n; and Eisenhower, 44–45, 48, 113–114; and EOU, 43; and Hughes, 141 n–143 n; March 31, 1944, memorandum of, 113–115; and marshalling yard attacks, 4–6, 56, 98; motivations of, 44–45; and oil attacks, 4, 32, 34, 37, 44, 52–56, 76, 84, 93, 96, 113–115, 148 n; status of, 49–50
Speer, Albert, 78, 157 n
Stalin, Joseph, 82
Stalingrad, 20
Stark, Andrew, 122, 128
Submarines, 24, 106–107
Surdon, 128, 132
Swinton, Ernest, 17–18

Tanks, 31, 148 n
Target selection, 20–23, 99–104, 107–110, 143 n–144 n. *See also* Bridge attacks; Marshalling yard attacks; Oil attacks
Tedder, Arthur William, 5, 35, 77, 88, 112, 139 n, 141 n, 146 n–147 n; background of, 15, 141 n; and bridge attacks, 56, 65, 151 n, 156 n; and Eisenhower, 46–47; and marshalling yard attacks, 3–4, 13–14, 46–47, 80, 84, 88–91, 96–98, 141 n, 154 n–155 n; and Mediterranean campaign, 38–39, 45, 75, 148 n; and oil attacks, 52–56, 148 n; status of, 49, 66; and Zuckerman, 7, 9, 13
Tergnier, 135
Thouers, 124–125
Thury Harcourt, 126
Toulouse, 125
Tours, 135
Toynbee, Arnold, 150 n

Transport plan. *See* Marshalling yard attacks
Tripoli, 9
Twenty-first Army Group, 62, 136
Tyson, James, 145 n

ULTRA, 21, 52, 61
U.S. Army Air Forces, 16, 19, 25–27, 44, 49
U.S. Embassy, 15, 142 n, 155 n
U.S. Strategic Bombing Survey, 155 n
USSTAF (U.S. Strategic Air Forces), 3, 32, 142 n, 144 n, 146 n, 154 n

Vandenberg, Hoyt S., 63, 151 n–152 n
V-E Day, 79–80
Vernon, 59, 61, 64, 75, 116–118, 151 n
Versailles, 126, 130
Vierzon, 127
Villedieu, 125
Vimoutiers, 127
Vire, 127
Vitre, 127
Voronezh, 20

War Department, U.S., 142 n
War Office, U.K., 3–4, 18, 39, 50, 69, 93
Webster, Charles, 30, 81–82, 139 n–140 n, 148 n, 157 n
Whitmore, William F., 73–74, 150 n, 155 n–156 n
Winant, John C., 17, 142 n
World War, First, 17

Zuckerman, Solly, 46, 74, 112, 139 n–141 n, 149 n, 154 n, 156 n; background of, 7–13; and bridge attacks, 56, 62, 64, 140 n–141 n, 151 n; and Kindleberger, 74, 139 n; and Leigh-Mallory, 7, 13–14; and marshalling yard attacks, 9–12, 13–14, 36–37, 155 n; and Mediterranean campaign, 38–39, 75; and Tedder, 7, 9, 13